'Terry Johnson has done it ag[...]
When Grace Comes H[...]
transforming grace looks lik[...]
following Jesus' own description of his disciples in the Beatitudes. What a
timely emphasis for a generation long on license and short on character.'

J. Ligon Duncan III
Senior Minister, First Presbyterian Church,
Jackson, Mississippi
Council, Alliance of Confessing Evangelicals

'A magnificent interpretation of the Beatitudes alongside that of Martyn
Lloyd-Jones, Sinclair Ferguson, John Stott and James Montgomery Boice,
to name only the more recent ones. My "Sermon on the Mount' note book
is now crammed with Johnsonisms—pithy one-liners that get to the
heart of what Jesus meant by adorning the righteousness of the kingdom
of God. Those who know him as I do can 'hear' him preach these powerful
and convicting sentences. This is where preaching and teaching needs to go.
A marvelous book which I cannot recommend too highly.'

Dr. Derek W. H. Thomas
Professor of Systematic and Practical Theology,
Reformed Theological Seminary, Jackson, Mississippi

'An older generation of Christians used to say, 'All truth is unto godliness.'
That is, all they learned from the Bible was meant to shape their lives for
God. The present generation of Christians increasingly struggles to know
what godliness looks like and how it can be found. In these pages Terry
Johnson takes us into Christ's answer to those questions as found in the
Beatitudes in the Sermon on the Mount. He explains and applies them
with a freshness that must surely fire every reader with the passion for the
true godliness that is so hard to find these days, yet which is so vital to
genuine Christian living.'

Mark G. Johnston
Grove Chapel, Camberwell

'Among Bible expositors there are dancers who dazzle the mind and diggers who dissect the heart, and while it is the dancers who excite, the diggers are the ones who edify. Terry Johnson is a digger, and his businesslike exploration of the Beatitudes is a clarion call to discipleship in depth.'

J. I. Packer
Professor of Theology, Regent College, Vancouver

'Only a lover and student of Holy Scripture who is also an experienced and caring pastor could have written this book. The Beatitudes have found, in Terry Johnson, the expositor we have all been waiting for, and they become, in his hands, a statement of Christian ethics as profound as it is readable. He is as faithful in bruising as in uplifting, but, being a true pastor, even his bruises have a velvet and healing touch.'

Alec Motyer

'Terry Johnson's sporting heroes are American, his spiritual mentors clearly English, especially John Stott. The exposition of the Beatitudes is a challenge to Christian counter-culture on both sides of the Atlantic. The Sermon on the Mount is a guide 'When Grace Transforms' and this book highlights one important part of those guidelines.'

Philip H. Hacking

When Grace Transforms :

The Character of Christ's Disciples Envisioned in the Beatitudes

by

Terry L . Johnson

Christian Focus Publications

© Terry L Johnson
ISBN 1 85792 770 2

Published in 2002
by
Christian Focus Publications Ltd,
Geanies House, Fearn,
Ross-shire, IV20 1TW,
Great Britain

www.christianfocus.com

Cover design by Alister Macinnes

Printed and bound by Mackay's of Chatham

Contents

Dedication

For my revered teachers in England who lived and taught the Beatitudes, and whose examples continue to provide daily inspiration,

James I. Packer
J. Alec Motyer

Preface

It was a different era. Growing up in Southern California in the 1950's and 60's, my sports heros were Sandy Koufax of the Dodgers and Jerry West of the Lakers. Koufax's six years from 1961–66 were perhaps the greatest half-dozen seasons of any pitcher in the history of baseball. West, "Zeke from Cabin Creek" as he was fondly called, was regarded by many as the greatest shooting guard in the history of professional basketball. Like most the athletes of that era they never drew attention to their accomplishments. Koufax looked embarassed when he struck out opposing batters. West always minimized his role in Laker victories, directing attention to his teammates. The contrast with today's attention grabbing, taunting, self-promoting, glory-seeking athletes is stark. Mickey Mantle looked at the ground when he rounded the bases after hitting a home run lest he humiliate the pitcher he had just victimized. Today's athlete points at himself *with both index fingers* as he jogs around the ball diamond.

Sandy Koufax is a Jew. If Jerry West is a Christian, neither he nor anyone else ever mentioned it. Their humility merely reflected the culture. Christian virtues had permeated the culture and stamped their image even upon the unbelieving. It was a different era. My how things have changed!

Today even the Christian world is confused about traditional Christian virtues. Self-promoting preachers lead self-indulgent congregations. Discipline, restraint, humility, sobriety, industry, and frugality are passé. Carnality and worldliness, ostentation and excess are typical. Back then, the Christian faith put its stamp on the culture. Now, the culture puts its stamp upon the

Christian community. The two can hardly be distinguished. The poor in spirit, those who mourn and the meek are nowhere to be found. David Wells' title says it all—we are *Losing Our Virtue*.

What does Christian virtue look like? What is the character of the Christian and how is he distinguished from the world? In the Sermon on the Mount in general and the Beatitudes in particular we are treated to Jesus' most complete description of his disciples. Jesus works from the inside out, zeroing in on the heart and describing the behavior that flows from it. What emerges is an individual, and then a community that is radically different. Transformed from within, the disciple of Christ "not like them," distinctive in moral purity, love for others, piety, faith, and eternal outlook. The key to it all is announced from the beginning, the Beatitudes, the virtues of the heart. They are strong medicine for our times, yet clearly just what the doctor ordered. If the Christian community is to witness as light and salt in the world rather than blending in with it, renewed study of the Beatitudes is the need of our times.

* * * * * * *

Matthew's Gospel is divided into five major teaching blocks, each of which concludes with the same formula ('when Jesus had finished...'). They are as follows:

5:1–7:29 Sermon on the Mount
10:5–11:1 Commissioning of the Twelve
13:1-53 Parables of the Kingdom
18:1–19:1 Various Teachings
24:1–26:1 Olivet Discourse

The block, 5:1–7:29, was first called 'the Sermon on the Mount' by Augustine of Hippo, the greatest of the church Fathers. It is, without doubt, the single most outstanding, most profound, most useful, and most influential sermon ever preached. In it we find the Beatitudes, our current concern, and also the Lord's Prayer, such warnings as 'you cannot serve God and mammon' and 'judge not lest you be judged' (6:24; 7:1), the command to 'seek first the kingdom of God and His righteousness (6:32), the invitation 'ask and you shall receive' (7:7), the Golden Rule (7:12), and the parable of the wise man who built his house upon the rock (7:24-27). The Puritan Thomas Watson says that we find in the Sermon on the Mount 'a breviary of religion,' 'the Bible epitomized,' 'a garden of delight,' and a 'conduit of the Gospel' (5). A lifetime of study would not be enough to plumb the depths of the Sermon.

There are two debates with respect to the title 'The Sermon on the Mount'. The first has to do with whether or not this collection of teachings can be called a sermon. Because some of the content of the 'sermon' is found in other contexts, certain commentators have drawn the conclusion that Matthew is employing a literary device in order to bring together in one body things Jesus taught throughout His ministry. They also point to the length of the material, as well as the diversity, as casting further doubt that there was such a singular sermonic occasion. But there is no compelling reason to doubt Matthew's version of things. Verses 1 and 2 certainly present this material as a single sermon.

> And when He saw the multitudes, He went up
> on the mountain; and after He sat down, His
> disciples came to Him. And opening His mouth
> He began to teach them, saying (Matt. 5:1,2).

Similarly the conclusion looks like the ending of an address:

> The result was that when Jesus had finished these
> words, the multitudes were amazed at His
> teaching; for He was teaching them as one having
> authority, and not as their scribes
> (Matt. 7:28,29).

9

Morris asks the right question in wondering, 'whether some commentators have paid sufficient attention to the fact that an itinerant preacher normally makes repeated use of his material, often with minor or even major changes' (92). That very similar things are said on very different occasions should not surprise us. No doubt Jesus taught the same things over and over. As for length, it may be that this 'sermon' was an extended teaching session, as was the case on other occasions, that stretched into several days (cf. 15:32).

The second issue has to do with whether it was delivered on a literal mount, or whether Matthew's reference to going up on the mountain has larger symbolic significance. Some commentators point out that there are no 'mountains' in Galilee, and so would see in this an implicit reference to Moses and Sinai, and the giving of a new Law. Others have rebutted that *oros*, mountain, may refer to the hill country west of the Sea of Galilee, and that such an allusion, if intended, is obscure. But it seems to me that some point of contact with Moses is intended, given the overall context of Matthew and the prominence that he has given to the theme of Jesus as the true Israelite. He has already drawn parallels between these themes in the life of the nation of Israel and events in the life of Jesus:

Exodus from Egypt (2:15)
Baptism in the Jordan (3:13-17; cf. 1 Cor. 10:1-3)
Temptation in the Wilderness (4:1-11)
Return from Exile (4:14-16)

Matthew may be drawing parallels between Jesus on the 'Mount' and Moses at Mount Sinai. Moses went up the mountain to receive and then deliver the Law. Jesus goes up the mountain to deliver the Law of the kingdom. Moses' Law is the rule of life for the people of God. Likewise Jesus' sermon provides the rule of life for the people of God. Jesus has 'absorbed the Mosaic function,' says Davies (quoted in Hill, 109). At least at some level, Jesus is the new Moses who rightly interprets and applies the Law of God for the people of God (cf. Matt. 5:17-48). 'It seems likely,' says Stott, 'that he deliberately went up to the mountain to teach, in order to draw a parallel between Moses who received the Law at Mount Sinai and himself...' (20). We may conclude it is a sermon, it was delivered from the 'mount,' and that Jesus is functioning in a Moses-like manner.

How it Functions

How is the teaching of the Sermon, in general, and the Beatitudes, in particular, to function in the life of the people of God? There have been any number of opinions offered over the years. We need to identify and refute several of them before we move on to the more likely view.

First the Sermon does not provide an ethos whereby the kingdom of God might be established. Jesus is not saying, as the social-gospellers of a previous generation thought He was, that the kingdom will be established as we go out and live according to the Sermon on the Mount. It was treated by them as a 'moral road map toward social progress,' as Carson put it (126). We can end war, eliminate ignorance and poverty, solve crime, banish hunger, and so on, if only we will apply the Sermon on the Mount, they said. Already by 1958, after two world wars, Lloyd-Jones was saying of this view that 'we do not need to waste time with it.' He regarded it as 'utterly ridiculous' (I, 13). The natural man has no ability or inclination to live by the Sermon on the Mount. Similarly, Jesus is not saying, 'go and do these things and you will become a Christian.' It is not a new legalism by which to reform or regenerate humanity. I do not become a Christian by adopting the ethic of the Sermon on the Mount nor can we create a Christian world by persuading the world to live by the Sermon on the Mount.

Second, the Sermon does not provide an ethic for a futuristic kingdom age. This was taught by the old dispensationalists, such as Lewis Sperry Chafer, H.A. Ironsides, J. Vernon McGee, and the Schofield Reference Bible. They argued that the ethics taught in the Sermon on the Mount are the ethics of a kingdom offered by Jesus to the Jews but rejected by them. This led to a suspension of the ingdom, the replacement of it by the church age, which remains until the millennium when the kingdom with its ethic will be reinstituted. The ethics of the Sermon on the Mount, they would say, have nothing to do with the church. So many objections have been raised to this view that later dispensationalists such as Ryrie, Walvoord, and Dwight J. Pentecost, have modified it, arguing that the ethics of the Sermon are binding in every age. But they still drive a wedge between the Sermon and the gospel. They point out that Jesus does not mention in these chapters the cross, justification by faith, new birth, and so on. 'On this basis,' Carson notes, 'the Epistle of James is also non-Christian' (127).

Third, the right view then is that the Sermon on the Mount 'shows us what life is like in the kingdom of God,' as Morris puts it (92). It does not show us how to earn or merit salvation, 'but when we have received this salvation as God's free gift,' Morris continues, 'the sermon shows us how we should live in the service of our gracious God'(92).

The fundamental graciousness of the Sermon should not be missed. We have noted above the parallels with Sinai and the Law. We should not miss the discontinuities as well. Matthew Henry notes the similarities saying, 'Christ preached this sermon, which was an exposition of the Law, upon a mountain, because upon a mountain the Law was given; and this was also a solemn promulgation of the Christian Law. But,' he continues, 'observe the difference:'

> ... when *the law was given*, the Lord *came down* upon the *mountain*; now the Lord *went up*: then, he spoke *in thunder and lightning*; now, *in a still small voice*: then the people were ordered to keep their distance; now they are invited to draw near: a blessed change!

The Sermon on the Mount begins with blessings. Repeatedly Jesus punctures the claims of self-righteousness (see especially 5:21-48; 6:1-18; 7:1-5). God-wrought heart change is assumed necessary throughout. 'It is significant that this sermon begins with Beatitudes rather than imperatives,' says Morris. 'Jesus will go on to make great demands on His followers, but these demands are to be understood in a context of grace' (95).

John R.W. Stott, in his wonderful commentary, *The Message of the Sermon on the Mount,* says of the Sermon, 'it depicts the behavior which Jesus expected of each of his disciples,' describing 'what human life and human community look like when they come under the gracious rule of God' (24,18). J.C. Ryle finds answers in the Sermon on the Mount to such questions as 'what kind of people Christians ought to be...the character at which Christians ought to aim...the outward walk and inward habit of mind which becomes a follower of Christ' (32).

Jesus repeatedly makes these points by contrasting the ways of His disciples with those of the world, as exhibited by either pagan Gentiles or Pharisees. As Stott points out, one could almost take the phrase, 'do not be like them' (6:8), as the theme for the whole presentation. Do not pray like them, do not fast like them, do not give like them, do not eagerly seek material things like them, says Jesus in chapter 6. The followers of Jesus are to be different. Nowhere are the distinctive beliefs and practices of Christians more clearly spelled out and contrasted with the world than here.

The Particulars

Perhaps now we are ready to look at these particulars. The Sermon on the Mount provides the larger context for our understanding of the Beatitudes. What are the specific characteristics of God's people as described there? We will essentially follow the structure outlined by Stott with some alterations.

First, Jesus discloses the character of His disciples (5:3-12).

What are the internal, heart qualities of the people of God? The Beatitudes describe them. Those who are the 'blessed' and favored of God are exactly the opposite of what the casual observer might think. It is not the popular, not the powerful, not the proud. Even today we tend to interpret material or worldly success as a sign of God's blessing. Rather, it is the 'poor in spirit' who inherit the kingdom of heaven. This underscores the essential graciousness of God's kingdom. Those who go to heaven, as we might put it, are not the 'great ones.' They're not even those who have accomplished great things for God, or participated in the right religious ceremonies and rituals, or who have performed the requisite moral works. Who are they? They are those characterized by poverty of spirit. In other words, it is those who are humble and broken before God, who know they are sinners, and who meekly seek His mercy (v 5). They don't play at religion, or trifle with spiritual things. They don't have to be coerced into coming to church, or reading Christian literature, or praying, because they 'hunger and thirst after righteousness' (v 6). They are merciful (v 7). They are pure in heart (v 8). They are peacemakers (v 9). And they are persecuted for their troubles, though even in this they rejoice (vv 10-12). By the grace of God they have been transformed. God's kingdom is open to, it is composed of, and it is characterized by those who humbly and meekly seek after God. This is all that God asks of us, Jesus would have us know. He seeks not great gifts or great exertions. He is concerned primarily with our hearts. Those who humble themselves, confess their sin, and pursue righteousness, whatever their background, whatever their prior sins, whatever their socio-economic status, are the ones blessed by God.

Second, Jesus explains the influence of His disciples that flows from these Beatitudes (5:13-16).

They are the 'salt of the earth.' They are the 'light of the world.' The influence of His disciples flows from their character. Because they are what they are they have the influence that they do. They do not blend into the world but are distinctive from it. Like salt they purify and preserve. Like light they dispel the darkness of error and falsehood. Thus they have a sanctifying effect on the world. The world is a better place for their having been there. They provide a model, an example for others of love and mercy. Their work ethic stands out in the market-place. Their marriages are exceptionally strong. Their child-rearing practices typically result in children who are exceptionally well behaved, secure, and happy. The world respects and admires the way of life of God's people and says, 'we want to be as they are.' Thus the salt permeates. This is the light that shines.

Third, Jesus speaks of the righteousness of His disciples (5:17-48).

What is the Christian's relationship to the Law of God? Is he free from the Law's moral requirements? As has always been the case, New Testament and Old Testament, he is free from the Law as a means of justification (Gal. 3:6-25; Rom. 3:19-4:25; 8:1-4). But Christians are expected to keep the Law as a means of pleasing the One who gave it and whose holiness it expresses. Jesus said that He did not come to 'abolish' the Law or prophets but to 'fulfill' (5:17). He says the Law remains normative for the life of the people of God in this era and until 'heaven and earth pass away' (5:18).

Further, their righteousness must 'surpass that of the scribes and Pharisees' if they are to enter the kingdom of heaven (5:20). They cannot be content with a legalistic conformity to the Law of God, settling for an external, superficial application of the letter of the Law while violating its deeper, spiritual intent. For Christ's disciples, it will not be enough not to murder – they mustn't hate. It will not be enough not to commit adultery – they mustn't lust. It will not be enough not to vow falsely – they must always speak the truth. Their yes must be yes and their no, no. It will not be enough merely to love their neighbour...and hate their enemy. They must love their enemy as well. The standard for their behavior is God Himself, not what those around them are doing. It is not enough for Christian disciples to be good relative to other people. They must 'be perfect' as their heavenly Father is perfect (5:48).

Fourth, Jesus describes the piety of His disciples (6:1-18).

How do disciples of Christ go about exercising the disciplines which nurture and express devotion to God? The first thing to notice is that there are such. Jesus assumes that His disciples practice the disciplines which nurture piety. This doesn't mean that He deals with those disciplines exhaustively, or that all the disciplines are included here. But it is clear that we are expected to practice spiritual disciplines. He gives three examples. How do we give our contributions? How do we pray? How do we fast? John Stott summarizes Jesus' response: 'In their "piety" or religious devotion Christians are to resemble neither the hypocritical display of the Pharisees nor the mechanical formalism of pagans' (25). We are not to 'sound a trumpet' when we give or pray or fast, 'in order to be seen by men' (6:2,5,16). We are to give and pray and fast 'in secret' and our Father 'who sees in secret' will repay us (6:4,6,18). When we pray we are not to babble on and on with 'meaningless repetition,' but pray after the manner of that most famous of all prayers, the 'Our Father,' which Jesus now teaches His disciples (6:9-13). Christian people are characterized by private and deeply personal devotion to God, wherein they give and fast and pray to God as to a Father. They do this not because it is a legal requirement, nor for the sake of show, but out of love.

16

We see here the balance for which we are to strive and which Jesus commands. The disciplines alone are worthless. But one does not therefore abandon them. Rather, one exercises them with the right motive and attitude. Jesus handles tithing in the same way. He condemns the tithing practice of the Pharisees not because there was a defect in the discipline itself. No, He tells them, 'these are the things you should have done.' You should tithe even down to the 'mint and dill and cummin.' But you ought not to do so to the neglect of the weightier provisions of the Law' such as 'justice and mercy and faithfulness' (Mt 23:23). The answer then is not to throw out the disciplines but to be sure to exercise them as a means of grace, as a means of knowing, loving, and serving God, not as ends in themselves.

Fifth, Jesus describes His disciples' life of faith (6:19-7:6).

'The worldliness which Christians are to avoid can take either a religious or secular shape,' Stott notes again. 'So we are to differ from non-Christians not only in our devotions, but also in our ambitions' (25). Christ utterly transforms our outlook on material wealth. We are to trust in the provision of God for our material well being. We lay up treasures not on earth, but in heaven (6:19,20). We serve God not money (6:24). Unlike pagans who are utterly preoccupied with what they will eat, drink, and clothe themselves, Christians are to be free from these material anxieties (6:25ff.). Neither are they to be concerned with what others are doing or saying, nor about specks in the eyes of others while logs remain in their own (7:1-6). Instead they 'seek first' the kingdom of God. The honor and glory of Christ is their first ambition, their first priority (6:33).

Sixth, He explains the Christian's commitments (7:7-29).

The Sermon on the Mount concludes with exhortations to commitment.

The first commitment is to earnest prayer (7:7-11). Prayer to our Father is presented as the means through which we may obtain the virtues described in the Beatitudes and throughout the Sermon. We are to 'ask,' 'seek,' and 'knock.' Jesus speaks of prayer 'as the appointed means of attaining what we need, especially grace to obey the precepts He had given,' says Matthew Henry. Our dependence upon God and need of His gracious transforming power is demonstrated by placement of this call to prayer at the conclusion of the Sermon on the Mount.

The second commitment is to simple obedience. We are to live by the 'Golden Rule,' doing to others as we would have them do to us (7:12).

One sign of genius is the ability to take very complex things and explain them very simply. Jesus captures in this statement a simple principle by which to govern all relationships: do to others as you would have them do to you.

The third commitment is to total commitment (7:13-29). We are called to commit ourselves to living by the words of Christ. This means entering the narrow gate and walking the narrow way (7:13,14). It means rejecting the false prophets who approximate the truth, who are like wolves in sheep's clothing, but may be known by their fruit (7:15-20). We are cautioned that not all who say 'Lord, Lord' will enter the kingdom of heaven. Many will claim to be Christ's disciples. Indeed some may even prophesy, cast out demons, and perform miracles in His name. Yet on judgment day will hear the terrible words, 'I never knew you' (7:23). Who are the true disciples? They are those who do the will of the Father (7:21); those who hear His words and 'act upon them,' building upon them as upon a rock, as compared to hearing and not acting upon them, building their lives, as it were, upon sand (7:24-27). Once again Stott summarizes so beautifully for us:

Thus the followers of Jesus are to be different – different from both the nominal church and the secular world, different from both the religious and the irreligious. The Sermon on the Mount is the most complete delineation anywhere in the New Testament of the Christian counter-culture. Here is a Christian value-system, ethical standard, religious devotion, attitude to money, ambition, life-style and network of relationships – all of which are totally at variance with those of the non-Christian world. And this Christian counter-culture is the life of the kingdom of God, a fully human life indeed but lived out under the divine rule.

Matthew tells us,

> The result was that when Jesus had finished these words, the multitudes were amazed at His teaching; for He was teaching them as one having authority, and not as their scribes (Matt. 7:28,29).

They were amazed and we are amazed. His teaching has authority. His words cannot merely be ignored. Jesus forces a decision. Every generation must face the force of these words, and either acknowledge their divine authority or reject them. They are the context of our study.

The Beatitudes are Jesus' description of the unique character of His disciples. We are ready now to give them our attention and embrace them as our own.

1

Introducing The Beatitudes

The disciples of Jesus are not to be like or live like the rest of the world. As we have seen Jesus maps out the difference in the Sermon on the Mount. 'Do not be like them,' He says (6:8). They are to be characterized by different *virtues*, the Beatitudes (5:1-12); a different *standard* of righteousness, exceeding the external and superficial legalism of the scribes and Pharisees, instead being perfect like their heavenly Father (5:16-48); a different *piety*, not practicing their righteousness before men but in secret (6:1-18); a different *outlook*, trusting God by laying up treasures in heaven not on earth, and seeking first the kingdom of God (6:19–7:6); and different *commitments*, praying earnestly, and building their lives upon the words of Christ, as upon a rock (7:13-29), and results in their being a sanctifying influence, like salt and light (5:13-16).

We have looked closely at the *context* of the Beatitudes, the Sermon on the Mount. Now we are ready to look at the Beatitudes themselves. The Sermon is prefaced by eight virtues that characterize the disciple of Christ. These virtues are traditionally called Beatitudes, from the Latin *beatitudo*, meaning 'blessed.' 'Blessed' should probably not be translated 'happy,' as some have suggested. Morris points out that whereas 'happy' brings out the secular content of joy, it does not do justice to the religious dimension. 'Happy,' says Carson, 'will not do for the Beatitudes, having been devalued in modern usage' (131). Happiness, as popularly understood, is associated too closely with positive circumstances and superficial excitement. Yet we would not wish to argue against older commentators such as Jeremiah Burroughs who summarizes the Beatitudes as describing *The Saints' Happiness*, that is, his true happiness, his happiness rightly understood. 'The Sermon on the Mount says... if you really want to be happy, here is the way,' says Lloyd-Jones. 'This and this alone is the type of person who is truly happy' (32).

Even so, 'blessed' (*makarios*) is probably better represented by the English words 'favored' and 'approved.' It represents a state of being, a status in relation to God rather than a subjective condition of the heart. The meaning is, 'these are the blessed of God,' these are the ones with whom God is pleased, not, 'these are the ones who have pleasant feelings.' 'It is not a psychological description,' says France (108). 'Singularly favored by God,' is Carson's understanding of *makarios* (131). France favors 'fortunate' or 'well-off' (108), Keener 'it will go well with the one who' (165). But the point of the term is to describe what God thinks of them, and does for them, not how they feel in response. Keener refers to the 'divine passives' in each of the Beatitudes and sees them as suggesting 'that God will provide these rewards directly; He will comfort them, bestow the earth, satisfy His people, show mercy, reveal Himself,' and so on (167).

Further, these eight virtues are descriptive of every Christian. Jesus is not describing the monastic or clerical few, or what Stott calls 'a small spiritual aristocracy remote from the common run of Christians' (31). These are not the characteristics of a spiritual elite. They are the qualities of all true Christians. Matthew Henry describes the Beatitudes as 'the principal graces of a Christian.' France finds in them an outline of 'the attitudes of the true disciple' and 'the best way of life' (109). Dodd argues that they 'describe the types of character which have God's approval' (in Hill, 110). Together, says Tasker, they 'make up the character of those who alone are accepted by the divine King as His subjects (3, 10)' (61). They are 'Christ's own specification of what every Christian ought to be. All these qualities are to characterize all his followers,' says Stott (31). 'Read the Beatitudes,' says Lloyd-Jones, 'and there you have a description of what every Christian is meant to be' (331). All true disciples of Christ are known by these Beatitudes. They describe 'the generality of Christian disciples, at least in the ideal,' adds Stott (38).

The commentators point out that the repetition of 'theirs' throughout the Beatitudes has an 'antithetical effect' (in the words of W.D. Davies). 'It is not reading too much into these verses to find that it is "these" people rather than "those" people who are blessed,' continues Davies (in Morris, p. 96 note 16). Only those who are characterized by these Beatitudes receive the approval, the favor, the blessing of God. There is no lesser order of believer also blessed by God. True believers are being described, and they alone, Jesus is saying, receive the kingdom of God.

Finally these eight virtues are qualities that are despised by the world. Jesus is turning worldly thinking on its head. He is demanding that we see things as God sees them. The world admires the proud, the strutting, the taunting, not the 'poor in spirit.' It demands its pound of flesh, not mercy. The meek? They're weak. Mourning? That would ruin the party. Peacemaking? Suffering persecution? These are not virtues to the world. These are weaknesses from which worldlings recoil. 'Let us learn how entirely contrary are the principles of Christ to the principles of the world,' says J.C. Ryle (34). Power, war-making, the ability to control, the ability to inflict pain – these are the qualities admired and sought by the world. The powerful, the wealthy, the influential often seem to be the ones who enjoy the approval of God. After all, His blessing has allowed them to enjoy the temporal prosperity which they possess, they might argue. But Jesus declares that things are not as they would appear. The first shall be last and the last first (Matt. 20:16). Rather it is the lowly, humble, suffering people of God who are the favored, the approved, the blessed by God.

We read the Beatitudes as ideals to which we are to aspire. They provide a portrait for us of the Christian. They describe the graces, the attitudes, the character qualities which please God and which He promises to bless. We are not to think that we can affect them by our own willpower or moral strength. He must give us hearts for Himself. Nevertheless they are the goal for which we are to 'ask,' 'seek,' and 'knock,' looking as we do for God to give them in gracious response.

2

Poor in Spirit

Let us look now at the first of these virtues so commended by Jesus, and so shunned by the world:

> Blessed are the poor in spirit, for theirs is the kingdom of heaven (Matt. 5:3).

Meaning

What does Jesus mean by the 'poor in spirit'? Luke records Jesus' words as 'blessed are the poor' (Lk. 6:20). Why the difference? Actually there is no difference. Matthew is merely elaborating. Matthew is giving us the divinely ordained interpretation of the meaning of Jesus' original Aramaic expression. By 'poor' He means not that material poverty is a blessing or that it leads to future blessing. The 'poor' who are often commended in the Old Testament are not those merely who lack material wealth. The 'poor' came to signify the righteous poor, those who are poor because of oppression and persecution, and yet continue to trust and obey God (see Ps. 34:6; Is. 41:17,18). By 'poor in spirit' Jesus means the 'spiritually poor,' that is, those who know that they have nothing and are nothing spiritually. Even as those who are physically poor are materially destitute, so also those who are spiritually poor are bereft of spiritual resources, and are humbly aware of their need.

Morris identifies the 'poor in spirit' as 'those who recognize that they are completely and utterly destitute in the realm of the spirit. They recognize their lack of spiritual resources and therefore their complete dependence on God' (95). Lloyd-Jones identifies it with the conviction of one's inability and hopelessness. He contrasts it with self-confidence, self-assurance, and self-reliance. Carson says to be poor in spirit 'is not to lack courage, but to acknowledge spiritual bankruptcy. It confesses one's unworthiness before God and utter dependence upon Him' (32). Stott says, 'to be poor in spirit is to acknowledge our spiritual poverty, indeed our spiritual bankruptcy, before God' (39).

Repeatedly the Scripture identifies poverty of spirit as a characteristic of God's most effective and most used servants. This is the spirit of Moses, who when called by God to lead his people out of Egypt said in response, 'Who am I, that I should go to Pharaoh, and that I should bring the sons of Israel out of Egypt?' (Ex. 3:11). This is the spirit of Gideon, who when asked by God to deliver his people from the Midianites, said, 'O Lord, how shall I deliver Israel? Behold, my family is the least in Manasseh, and I am the youngest in my father's house' (Judg. 6:15). This is the spirit of David, who when promised by God that he would establish his kingdom forever, said, 'Who am I, O Lord God, and what is my house, that Thou hast brought me this far?' (2 Sam. 7:18). This is the spirit of Isaiah, who when granted a vision of God sitting on His throne 'lofty and exalted,' with the seraphims calling out to one another saying, 'Holy, holy, holy, is the Lord God of hosts, the whole earth is full of His glory,' cries out 'woe is me, for I am ruined! Because I am man of unclean lips and I live among a people of unclean lips; for my eyes have seen the King, and the Lord of hosts' (Is. 6:5). This is the spirit of Jeremiah, who when God said to him, 'I have appointed you a prophet to the nations,' answered 'Alas, Lord God! Behold, I do not know how to speak, Because I am a youth' (Jer. 1:5,6). This is the spirit of Peter, who when the reality of Christ's divinity first pressed in upon his conscience, cried out and said, 'depart from me for I am a sinful man!' (Lk. 5:8). In each of these cases there is a profound sense of weakness, and inability, and inadequacy. Does this not contrast sharply with the proud, self-confident ideal of our world today? You can do it, the world says. You can accomplish anything you set your mind to do. The servants of God say, 'How can I do that? I'm too young, or inexperienced, or inarticulate, or sinful, or ordinary.'

Nowhere is this more clearly seen than in the Apostle Paul, who can say, 'I know that nothing good dwells in me' (Rom. 7:18). Again he says, 'for I am the least of all the apostles, who am not fit to be called an apostle' (1 Cor. 15:9). He identifies himself as 'the chief of sinners' (1 Tim. 1:15), 'the very least of all saints' (Eph. 3:8), and a 'nobody' (2 Cor. 12:11). How could he minister if this was how he saw himself, one might ask today. He has such a poor self-image, such low self-esteem. He tells us himself, 'by the grace of God I am what I am' (1 Cor. 15:10). Indeed this poor 'self-image' is the key to his effective service. When God further weakened him with a 'thorn in the flesh,' Paul was given the insight, 'My grace is sufficient for you, for power is perfected in weakness.' (2 Cor. 12:9). Because he was weak and inadequate He looked to God for help, and consequently was enabled to do what he would not otherwise have been able to do. 'When I am weak,' he says, 'then I am strong' (2 Cor. 12:10). He can cry out, who is adequate for these things,' and answer, 'our adequacy is from God' (2 Cor. 2:16; 3:5). 'Most gladly, therefore, I will rather boast about my weaknesses, that the power of Christ may dwell in me,' he says (2 Cor. 12:9). We see this same spirit in the prodigal son, who says, 'Father, I have sinned against heaven and in your sight; I am no longer worthy to be called your son' (Lk. 15:21). It is this spirit that the gospel breeds. The conclusion of the argument of Romans 1–3 in which the Apostle Paul demonstrates the universality of human rebellion and sin is that 'every mouth may be closed' (Rom. 3:19). The poor in spirit are characterized by the closed mouth. They have no illusions about themselves.

They no longer are making any excuses. They are no longer rationalizing their behavior. They see themselves as they truly are. They are not making false claims about their virtue. They see the darkness of their own heart. They confess and admit that their hearts are 'deceitful above all else and desperately wicked' (Jer. 17:9). They know there is 'no good thing' in them either (Rom. 7:18). They see the smallness and the weakness and the poverty of their souls. In addition, they have no confidence in their flesh; they have no confidence in their ability to please God through their behavior. They acknowledge that all their good works are like filthy rags (Is. 64:6). With respect to the approval and the blessing of God, they have no confidence in their family background, their temperament, their charm, their power, their money, their wealth, their education, their personality, their intelligence, their morality, their conduct, their good behavior – nothing. They have no confidence in anything whatsoever. Why? Because they know themselves. They look into their hearts and see darkness. They look into their souls and they see poverty.

We can also identify the poor in spirit by contrasting them with their opposite. The Apostle John relays the words of Jesus with respect to the church of Laodicea. He says to them,

> Because you say, 'I am rich, and have become
> wealthy, and have need of nothing,' and you do
> not know that you are wretched and miserable
> and poor and blind and naked (Rev. 3:17).

Do you see their problem? They think that they are rich. They think that they are wealthy. They think that they have no need. But what is the reality? The reality is far different. The reality is that they are 'wretched and miserable and poor and blind and naked.' This is what we must know about ourselves. Let there be no illusions. Let us not be self-deceiving. Spiritual health requires that we acknowledge the spiritual wasteland that we are.

Promise

Does all this sound bleak? Well, of course it does. Jesus is standing the world upon its head. The world can't understand what is 'blessed' about this condition. But Jesus says the poor in spirit are 'blessed.' Those who know these things about themselves are approved and favored by God. Did you think that the accumulation of vast material wealth was a sign of God's favor? Oh no, God favors or blesses the poor in spirit. Jesus says, 'theirs is the kingdom of heaven'. Morris says, 'we should understand this in the sense of consequence rather than reward. In no sense do they merit the kingdom, but being what they are they possess it' (96). To whom does the kingdom of God belong? The kingdom of God belongs not to the powerful, not to the rich, not even to the self-righteously religious and moral. The kingdom of God is given freely to those who are utterly undeserving so long as they know themselves to be such. As we have seen, by 'theirs' we should understand 'theirs alone.' To whom is the kingdom of God given? To those who are humble enough to acknowledge their unworthiness to receive it. Who enjoys the favor of God? 'But to this one I will look,' God says, 'to him who is humble and contrite of spirit, and who trembles at my word' (Is. 66:2b). Again He says to us, 'For thus says the high and exalted One Who lives forever, whose name is Holy, 'I dwell on a high and holy place, and also with the contrite and lowly of spirit'(Is. 57:15a). This, the first of the Beatitudes, sets the tone for the whole sermon. The ethical demands of the Sermon on the Mount are not the conditions for entrance to the kingdom of God, that people can achieve themselves. Carson says, 'all must begin by confessing that by themselves they can achieve nothing' (122).

Notice as well that only this and the last of the Beatitudes is in the present tense. Jesus' meaning is that the kingdom of God, or the 'rule' of God is something that one begins to possess even now. He certainly means that in receiving the kingdom one's soul is eternally saved. But He also means

29

that one enters into the benefits of God's kingdom while still here on earth, though admittedly the completeness of that rule and the completeness of the blessings are not realized until the consummation at the end of time. Thus, to be 'poor in spirit' is a blessing both now and in eternity. It is a blessing not just because one's soul is saved in eternity, but because there are benefits, psychological and otherwise, to be received even in the present tense. Why would that be? Because poverty of spirit is an outlook that gets one in touch with reality. One comes to truly know one's self and in knowing oneself also to know God. To know that one is the 'chief of sinners' or 'the least of all the saints' or a 'nobody' is not a depressing or discouraging realization, rather a liberating one. One might compare it to a medical affliction that cannot be explained. One has a lump, or a fever, or an elevated white blood cell count and no one can discover the cause. This can be frightening. One can try to carry on normally, but it is unmistakably there. When the report finally comes in that identifies the malady it is often greeted with a measure of relief. 'At least we know what it is,' we say; 'now we can treat it.' But, you might counter, what if the report says that your condition is terminal? Then what? Well, that would be bad news indeed. But the gospel says just the opposite. It says, bad as your condition is, Jesus can cure you! Here is the truth about you, it says. It is terrible. It is awful. You are in much worse condition than you ever thought. Let's not sugar-coat it. You are hopeless. But Jesus can and will cure you, if only you will but ask. This is a great blessing.

But to live a false illusion of self-righteousness is a terrible burden to carry through life. One must essentially live a lie. One lives in a fantasy world of false images about one's alleged virtues and goodness. Yet one is always stumbling and falling and failing. One never really lives up to the fantasy. This requires explanations. So one blame-shifts or rationalizes. The soul is self-deceived. One carries about a great burden of guilt and unrealized expectations. But the one who is 'poor in spirit' knows the truth about himself and so in a sense can relax and be himself and be real. He knows his sins are forgiven and so he has peace of mind. He can be honest about failure. He can give thanks for progress that is made in subduing the flesh and in gaining victory over sin. He can delight in progress that is made in personal sanctification, in the refining of his personality, and the purging out of defects of character. When he fails, he is not shocked but merely realizes afresh the greatness of the grace of God that has preserved him in times of obedience and his continuing need of grace especially in times of failure. This is how the 'poor in spirit' begin to enjoy the benefits of God's kingdom in the present tense.

Means

How then do I get there? I wish to be poor in spirit. But I see my pride. I see my self-righteousness. I see my ego. How do I come to be the humble man who is blessed by God?

First, we must avoid the counterfeits of poverty of spirit.

There are false imitations of this virtue that we don't want confused with the real thing.

1. It is not natural diffidence.

There are folks who are born with unobtrusive personalities, who are naturally quiet and retiring. Jesus is not saying that God prefers one personality type over another. The Beatitudes are not natural qualities. Rather they are supernatural and Spirit-given. To be 'poor in spirit' is not to be born with a shy personality. There is no God-favored personality type. Some people are naturally loud and aggressive. Some are quiet and retiring. We mustn't make a virtue of one and a vice of the other. Those who are quiet are just as prone toward self-righteousness and pride as those who are loud, perhaps more so. I have noticed that loud-types are often penitent about their boisterousness, even ashamed

31

and embarrassed about their behavior, whereas the silent-type often sit back, look down their noses, and condemn everyone around them who is more active or aggressive than themselves. Natural reticence does not guarantee poverty of spirit.

2. *It is not false modesty.*

It is not me going around trying to convince myself and others that I have nothing to offer, that I am a nobody, with nothing to contribute, nothing to add, etc. You have heard this sort of thing, no doubt. So and so will go about bad-mouthing himself about his ignorance, his material poverty, his spiritual immaturity, his lack of talent and abilities. Typically there are two problems with this. First, it may be that one's self-deprecating talk is actually self-promoting. It is calculated to draw attention to oneself. Sometimes it may even be designed to attract the contrary response. 'Oh no,' people will say, 'you are very wise, and gifted, and mature, and add so much to our church,' and so on. Or it is designed to impress people with our humility so they'll say, 'My, isn't he humble!' Of course anything designed to attract attention to oneself cannot be poverty of spirit but rather the opposite. And anything designed to attract praise is the opposite.

The other problem with false modesty is that it is often dishonest, involving statements that are untrue and ungrateful, that fail to appreciate the gifts that God has given. The person who says, 'I have nothing to contribute, I have no gifts, I have no talents,' and so on, is not only falsely perceiving reality, in that he does have something to give, but is despising God's gifts. It is absurd, not to mention embarrassing, to hear a beautiful woman complain that she is plain, a great athlete speak of his clumsiness, a thin person complain of how heavy he/she is, and so on. Again the life of the Apostle Paul is instructive. The same man who says 'nothing good dwells in me' says 'Christ lives in me' (Rom. 7:18; Gal. 2:20). The same man who says 'I am the least of all the apostles,' says at the same time, 'I labored even more than all of them' (1 Cor. 15:9,10). The same man who calls himself 'the very least of all the saints' says that grace was given to him 'to preach to the Gentiles the unfathomable riches of Christ' (Eph. 3:8). The same man who says he is 'a nobody,' says at the same instant, 'in no respect was I inferior to the most eminent apostles' (2 Cor. 12:12). Though he clearly sees his lowliness and unworthiness in the sight of God, he does not regard God's gifts as of no consequence. He has, and we ought to have, 'sound judgment.' We are 'not to think more highly of (our)self than (we) ought to think; but to think so as to have sound judgment' (Rom. 12:3).

We are not to go about denying the reality of God's gifts in the name of humility. Every one of us has something to offer, to give, to contribute. Granted, some have more than others. But all have something. I recall J.I. Packer's response to Joni Earickson's question about what she could do as a quadriplegic to serve God. His answer: you can worship God. You feel as though your life is over? You have nothing to contribute? No, you can worship God. If you're tempted to regard that as inconsequential, think again. Nothing, absolutely nothing, is of greater eternal consequence than sincere and true worship offered to Almighty God. We can worship, we can pray, we can trust, even if we can't get out of bed.

Second, how do we become 'poor in spirit'?

If to be 'poor in spirit' is not to be naturally diffident or to be falsely modest, then how do I get find the real thing?

1. We become 'poor in spirit' through understanding the greatness of God.

The finite is humbled by the knowledge of the infinite. We see our poverty most clearly in the light of His glory. This is the key to Moses and Gideon and David and Isaiah and Peter. I must see God. Then this sight begins to work on me. I begin to see myself as a tiny drop of finite existence over against the great ocean of His infinity. I begin to see my insignificance. All the things about which I might have boasted are as nothing.

33

And I begin to see my dependence. I did not create myself. Whatever aptitudes or abilities I possess have been given to me. 'What a poor thing it is, this boasting of the things that are accidental and for which I am not responsible,' says Lloyd-Jones (I,51). 'What do you have that you did not receive,' Paul asks (1 Cor. 4:7). As I realize these things in the light of my Creator, the wind begins to go out of the sails of pride. I did not make myself. I cannot preserve my health. I cannot protect myself from bodily harm. I cannot even guarantee my next breath. I am utterly dependent upon God for everything. This is humbling. Perhaps I thought of myself as a 'self-made man'. I was proud of my achievements, or my ancestry and family, or my intelligence, or my physical prowess, or my wealth, or my charm or personality. But having come face to face with God, I realize my true weakness and my vulnerability. I have nothing to boast about. All that I have are God's gifts to me. How could I possibly be proud and haughty when all that I am and all that I have are the gifts of God's goodness, not because of some inherent quality in me? I am no better than anyone else.

2. We become 'poor in spirit' through understanding the holiness of God.

Like Isaiah before me, when I gaze upon His holiness, His purity, His righteousness, I come to realize my wickedness and need of a Savior. I come to see the darkness of my own heart. My mouth is closed. I stop making excuses. Self-confidence and self-sufficiency and self-righteousness are dashed against the rocks of His purity. I come to realize, with the saints before me, that there is no good thing in me, and I cry out, in weakness, and fear, and trembling, 'Lord be merciful to me a sinner.' And the Bible promises, 'a broken and contrite heart, O God, Thou wilt not despise' (Ps. 51:17).

3. We become 'poor in spirit' through understanding the grace of God.

To whom does God extend this saving and sanctifying grace? It is precisely those who have abandoned all prentetions of self-righteousness and are looking only to the Lord Jesus Christ, His 'blood and righteousness' as the hymn – writer put it, for salvation. The 'poor in spirit' look only to the cross where Christ 'bore our sins in his body' (1 Peter 2:24), where 'he became a curse for us' (Gal 3:13) , where 'he gave his life a ransom for many (Mark 10:45), where 'he who knew no sin became sin so that we might receive his righteousness in him' (2 Cor. 5:21). 'We are but poor sheep who have gone astray, each of us turning our own way, but the Lord has caused the iniquity of us all to fall upon him.' (Is. 53:6). The poor in spirit realize that one must die in their place, on our behalf, as their substitute; they realize that if they are to be redeemed it must be 'by his doing' (1 Cor. 1:30, if they are to be saved it must be by his grace, through his gift (Eph 2:8-9).

Wouldn't you like to know that you were blessed of God? Wouldn't you like to know that your sins were forgiven? That you possessed eternal life? That the kingdom of heaven was yours? The path to heaven is the path called humility. God is not looking for men of great achievement. He is looking for those who know their weakness, their inability, and unworthiness. Are you willing to acknowledge your inability to please God and your hopelessness? Are you willing to admit your sin? Are you willing to acknowledge your dependence upon God and need of Christ? To such, and such alone, the kingdom of God belongs.

3

Those Who Mourn

We have seen that the virtues of the Beatitudes are those which the world despises. They are often not regarded as virtues at all, but as things to be avoided, things from which to flee. They see no virtue in being poor in spirit, or meek, or persecuted. To regard these things positively is incomprehensible to the world. Nowhere is this more apparent than with this the second of the Beatitudes:

> Blessed are those who mourn, for they shall be comforted (Matt. 5:4).

How can the condition of mourning be a blessed condition? To 'mourn' is synonymous with being miserable. Who wants to be unhappy? Who wants to grieve? Indeed the whole world system is designed to avoid sadness at all costs – literally at all costs. The entertainment industry exists for one thing and one thing only – pleasure. Movies, television, radio, recordings, concerts, magazines, books are almost all entirely designed for our pleasure. They don't educate. They don't inform. They merely entertain. The sports industry grows every year. From season to season the heart of the nation moves from football to basketball to baseball at the amateur and professional levels. Recently hundreds of alternative sports have sprung up. Every four years we have the Olympics. Every three years we have World Cup Soccer. Year round there are tennis and golf. The list is endless. The money involved is astronomical. One baseball player recently turned down a multi-year $81 million contract. He was holding out for $100 million. Not $100,000. Not even $1 million or the extraordinary figure of $10 million. That $100 million represents a remarkable commitment to pleasure. We might even further distinguish a recreational industry. Every Sunday millions of people miss church because they are camping or hunting or fishing. The interstate highways are full of RVs and boats and jet-skies. The airports are jammed with vacationers heading for the slopes, or the beaches. Our civilization is devoted to fun. The ideal life, it seems, is one continual party. Drink hard, play hard, eat heartily, run to one entertainment event after another. Fun, fun, fun. Play, play, play. Run to the golf course, then to the lake, then to the game, then to the party, then drop exhausted into bed, and then get up and start all over again. This is our modern world. While every civilization has had its amusements, never has one had as many opportunities, and had so much time and money so widely accessible so as to make the fulfillment of its lusts possible. Did Hobbes say that life is nasty, short, and brutish? No more! The pain-free, sorrow-free life is at hand. Yet Jesus says, 'blessed are those who mourn.' Could anything be more contrary to the spirit of our age? Could anything more poignantly illustrate the contrast between the values of the world and those of God's kingdom? Could anything more distinctly contrast the disciple of Christ from the world? Jesus pronounces His curse on our pleasure mania. 'Woe to you who laugh now,' He says, 'for you shall mourn and weep' (Lk. 6:25). 'The mind of fools is in the house of pleasure,' Ecclesiastes warns (7:4). Paul said that the love of pleasure would be characteristic of the last days (2 Tim. 3:4). Entertainment has become an idol, and as such it obstructs true spiritual development. The recreation craze of our day is not harmless. It endangers our souls and the souls of our children.

But why mourning? Why should Christ's disciples mourn? And why is such mourning a blessing? These are the questions which we must now answer.

Generally Considered

The first thing we need to recognize is that Jesus is not referring to every kind of mourning. He is not speaking of the mourning of the wicked, or those who mourn the loss of earthly things. Jesus even has in mind 'a more fundamental kind of mourning' than simple bereavement, says Morris (97). He is not saying that all the people who have ever mourned the passing of a loved one will be comforted. The ungodly will mourn their loss into eternity and forever, and never recover. The mourning to which He refers parallels the poverty of which He spoke in the first beatitude. 'Just as "the poor" does not mean all who are in actual poverty,' says Plummer, 'so "those who mourn" does not mean all who happen to be lamenting' (63). Even as it was spiritual poverty that was blessed so also it is spiritual mourning that is blessed. 'It is not the sorrow of bereavement to which Christ refers, but the sorrow of repentance,' says John Stott (40,41). Or more broadly, it is sorrow for sin in all its consequences, for the corruption, ruin, heartbreak, devastation, and disgrace that results because of sin. We may perceive a progression in the Beatitudes. The disciple of Christ has an accurate self-awareness, and so is 'poor in spirit.' Seeing the sin that is at the root of his inability and unworthiness, he mourns its presence in his heart, and wherever he encounters it.

This means that there is a fundamental seriousness about the Christian life. I don't believe that there are any happier people in all the world than the people of God. I see more real joy in them, and more real enjoyment of this world, and more zest for life than anywhere else. Still, Christ's disciples are set apart from the world by their gravity and sobriety. The world may be light and silly and frivolous, but not the church. God's people have the issues of eternity in the forefront of their minds. They are consumed by the realities of God and

39

man, Christ and sin, heaven and hell. Consequently they are serious, sober, grave. This is not to be confused with being miserable, sullen, and cold. But neither can we abide in a sitcom world of foolishness. All the world wants to do is escape. It doesn't want to think serious thoughts. It refuses to consider life and death issues. That is too 'heavy.' Serious thoughts might interfere with 'serious' drinking or partying. But we know that there is a spiritual war going on, and we are fully engaged in that war, and the casualty rate is high.

Why We Mourn

First, we mourn because of the presence of evil in the world.

We see God being dishonored by rebellion, idolatry, and unbelief. We see human misery at every turn because of war, crime, greed, the breakdown of the family, selfishness, lust, jealousy, and so on. We can't be indifferent to this. We can't remain unmoved. It breaks our heart. It grieves our spirit. Our supreme example of this mourning is Jesus. He wept at the grave side of Lazarus, as he grieved the anomaly and tyranny of death (Jn. 11:35). He wept over Jerusalem's unbelief, saying,

> O Jerusalem, Jerusalem, who kills the prophets and stones those who are sent to her! How often I wanted to gather your children together, the way a hen gathers her chicks under her wings, and you were unwilling (Matt. 23:37; cf. Lk.19:41).

Jesus is 'a man of sorrows acquainted with grief' (Is. 53:3). Sorrow was characteristic of Jesus. We might say of someone that he was 'a man of peace,' and mean that he was characterized by peace or 'a peaceful man.' Similarly we might say of another that he was 'a man of violence,' and mean that he was characterized by violence or 'a violent man.' Isaiah said of the Suffering Servant that He would be 'a man of sorrow' or 'a sorrowful man,' noted for and characterized by sorrow. Lloyd-Jones points out that the New Testament never speaks of Jesus laughing. We read of His anger and His grief, but not laughter. Arguments from silence are weak, but nevertheless the omission is significant.

We see more of the same in the prophets and apostles. The Psalmist says,

> My eyes shed streams of water, because they do
> not keep Thy law   (Ps. 119:136).

He weeps 'streams of water' when he considers the lawlessness of the ungodly. Ezra's response to the unfaithfulness of Israel was to pray and make confession,'weeping and prostrating himself before the house of God' (10:1), saying,

> O my God, I am ashamed and embarrassed to lift
> up my face to Thee, my God, for our iniquities
> have risen above our heads, and our guilt has
> grown even to the heavens. Since the days of our
> fathers to this day we have been in great guilt, and
> on account of our iniquities...   (Ezra 9:6,7a)

Why was he 'weeping and prostrating himself'? Because of 'iniquities' and 'guilt' of his people. We are told of the Apostle Paul,

> Now while Paul was waiting for them at Athens,
> his spirit was being provoked within him as he
> was beholding the city full of idols (Acts 17:16).

Paul was 'provoked,' a word that includes a range of emotions from anger to grief. Because of what? Because he saw a city 'full of idols,' and was deeply disturbed by the sight. Elsewhere Paul chastises the Corinthians for their failure to grieve in the face of gross immorality, 'of such a kind as does not exist even among the Gentiles,' he said (1 Cor. 5:1). 'You have become arrogant, and have not mourned instead' (1 Cor. 5:2). Later he admitted to the Corinthians his fear that on his next visit,

> ...my God may humiliate me before you, and I may mourn over many of those who have sinned in the past and not repented of the impurity, immorality and sensuality which they have practiced   (2 Cor. 12:21).

He wouldn't be able to remain unmoved by such sin. He would 'mourn' over those who had 'not repented.' It would grieve him deeply. So he anticipates his response. Again he tells the Philippians of those who oppose the gospel:

> For many walk, of whom I often told you, and now tell you even weeping, that they are enemies of the cross of Christ   (Phil. 3:18).

The Apostle Paul weeps for the 'enemies of the cross.' He mourns their unbelief. This is a dimension of the Christian response to our world that we ought to ponder. Sometimes we argue among ourselves about our liberties, about where the line that separates non-sin from sin lies, and how close we can come to it without crossing over. The outlook of the second Beatitude all but invalidates that whole approach. The disciple of Christ is not flirting with sin, he is grieving over it. He does not find it alluring, he mourns it. He puts on the television, sees seductive images, hears Christian values mocked, and his heart is touched with sorrow. He sees teenage girls dressed for their proms like street walking harlots and he grieves the loss of innocence. He hears young children swearing and talking about trash and mourns the decline in public moral standards. He sees the soccer fields on the Lord's Day filled with oblivious youth and parents, and he shakes his head with sadness for the Sabbath that we've lost. He sees the reports of war, of crime, of violence; he sees the evidence of idolatry and immorality and injustice, and he is 'provoked.'

Is this you? I pray that we are not still blind to this. I pray that we are not still flirting with the world, attracted by its pleasures, seduced by its images. The worlding wants to know, what's the big deal? Lighten up, they say. What's the matter with showing a little skin, or with a few off-color jokes, or a few too many drinks, or a little fleshly indulgence or two, and so on. The child of God mourns these things. They break his heart.

Second, we mourn because of personal sin.

It isn't just the sin out there over which we grieve, but the sin in here, in our hearts. This is clear enough in the penitential Psalms (6,25,32,38,51,130), especially Psalm 51, written in the aftermath of David's sin with Bathsheba. But we also see it in the Apostle Paul who is clearly grief-stricken by his breeches in obedience, as revealed in Romans 7. He says,

> For that which I am doing, I do not understand; for I am not practicing what I would like to do, but I am doing the very thing I hate... For I know that nothing good dwells in me, that is, in my flesh; for the wishing is present in me, but the doing of the good is not... For the good that I wish, I do not do; but I practice the very evil that I do not wish (Rom.7:15,18,19).

Finally he cries out,

> Wretched man that I am! Who will set me free from the body of this death? (Rom. 7:24).

Some people make the mistake of saying that this is a Romans 7 problem and Paul (and we with him) graduate to Romans 8 and the empowering of the Holy Spirit and no longer have the problem of dealing with our wretchedness. But Paul goes on to say,

> And not only this, but also we ourselves, having the first fruits of the Spirit, even we ourselves groan within ourselves, waiting eagerly for our adoption as sons, the redemption of our body (Rom. 8:23).

'We ourselves groan within ourselves,' he says. In the era, in the period of time in which we have 'the first fruits of the Spirit,' and yet are 'waiting eagerly for our adoption,' we groan. Groaning is characteristic of life for Christians in this world. Why? In addition to the evil out there that grieves us, there are the problems within. We groan because of the struggle of Romans 7, the discrepancy between what we wish to be and what we are. We see that there is 'nothing good' in us and we groan. We see that we are doing 'the very thing (we) hate' and we groan. We suffer from the awareness of the gap between what we ought to be and what we are, and the resulting frustration, disappointment, and discouragement. For these things within us we mourn.

Third, we mourn because of the persecution we suffer.
Often this persecution has taken the form of violence or as is currently the case in our country, social ostracism. We discover that the world hates us even as it hated Christ, and we mourn (Jn. 15:18ff.). We mourn the loss of friends. We mourn the social rejection. 'In the world you will have tribulation,' Jesus said (Jn. 16:33). 'All who desire to live godly in Christ Jesus will be persecuted,' said the Apostle Paul (2 Tim. 3:12). For this we mourn.

Fourth, we mourn because of self-denial.
Christians suffer because they deny themselves things that other people enjoy. Some of these things are sinful pleasures that Christian discipleship forbids. While others may indulge in

immorality, gluttony, drunkenness, and the worship of mammon, living it up, enjoying the party, we are required to deny ourselves these things. There is no sense pretending that this isn't a form of suffering – it is. The pleasures of sin may last only a season, but they are nevertheless real. Hebrews tells us that Moses chose,

> rather to endure ill-treatment with the people of God, than to enjoy the passing pleasures of sin (Heb. 11:25).

The pleasures are 'passing pleasures,' but they are pleasures. Each time a child of God says 'no' to sin there is an emotional price, sometimes an agonizing price, that he pays. He suffers. He groans.

We are also required to deny ourselves things that otherwise might be legitimate. Why? For the sake of the gospel. We give up our rights and liberties for Christ's sake. 1 Corinthians 8–11 is full of this form of self-denial. The missionary gives up his liberty to enjoy material comfort in order to reach the lost. The eater of meat and drinker of wine gives up his liberty to do so in order to win those offended by such (Romans 14). Money is given that might have been kept. Time is given that might have been filled with leisure pursuits. Self-denial is an essential element of Christian discipleship. Jesus said,

> If anyone wishes to come after Me, let him deny himself, and take up his cross, and follow Me. For whoever wishes to save his life shall lose it; but whoever loses his life for My sake shall find it (Matt. 6:24,25).

To be a Christian is to practice self-denial for Christ's sake. It is our 'ambition' to be 'pleasing to Him' (2 Cor. 5:9). We live now no longer for ourselves 'but for Him who died and rose again' on our behalf (2 Cor. 5:15).

Fifth, we mourn in anticipation of eternity.

We long for a better world, but know we are locked in this fallen world. We were made for eternity but we are trapped in time. I remember an occasion when I was rocking my two-year-old to sleep. He was at a very cute, fun age. But I was hit with the awareness that this time would soon pass and be gone forever. I could not hold on to him or it. I cannot freeze time. We blink and it is gone. Loved ones pass away and they're gone. We can't hang onto them. They slip from our grasp. So we long for the eternal. We are 'waiting eagerly for our adoption as sons, the redemption of our body' (Rom. 8:23). 'For indeed,' Paul says, 'in this house we groan, longing to be clothed with our dwelling from heaven' (2 Cor. 5:2).

Both Lloyd-Jones and Stott point out that for too long Christian people have been denying this fundamental reality of Christian sorrow. The Christian life, says Stott, 'is not all joy and laughter.' He complains of those who 'seem to imagine that, especially if they are filled with the Spirit, they must wear a perpetual grin on their face and be continuously boisterous and bubbly' (41). This is not the case. As we have seen, there is a seriousness, a sobriety, and sorrow that is characteristic of the Christian life. There is a cross that God requires that we bear. A friend of mine, recently diagnosed with cancer, summed up the challenge of the Christian life, in this way:

> Up to the time I became a Christian, my life seemed to make sense. I had to work hard to achieve success in my career and my family-life. Life was pretty simple and seemed manageable. However, ever since I became a Christian, life has been full of paradoxes and enigmas. I must die in order to live; I must lose my life in order to find it: let the rich man glory in his poverty and the poor man glory in his riches; as Jim Elliot said, 'It is no fool who gives up what he cannot

keep to gain that which he cannot lose.' This makes no sense from a physical perspective, but from the eye of faith we see just a few glimpses of what God is talking about.

I have to admit that after twenty-five years of walking with the Lord I am still very much in the dark. The longer I live the more I realize that there is precious little that I am able to fully understand or much less control. I don't understand heaven, and those who say they do are dreaming. If we did understand heavenly things we would not need faith. All I can do is hold on to the few certainties which we do 'know.' I agree with Job, 'I know that my Redeemer liveth and will stand on the earth on the last day.' I can't fully comprehend Him but I trust Him. I am cynical and skeptical about human goodness, for He has said that there is no one good not even one, but I 'know' that he is all goodness, wisdom, justice, and mercy all at the same time. I 'know' that His love for me is unparalleled. No human love comes even close, and I certainly can't love others the way He loves me! It is His love which is the ROCK upon which I stand. Everything else is shifting sand.

Our Comfort

The Psalmist says,

> My life is spent with sorrow, and my years with sighing (Ps .31:10).

Yet Jesus promises that those who so mourn 'shall be comforted.' They will receive divine encouragement. Their sorrows shall be relieved. There is also a sense in which Jesus is indicating vindication. We mourn because of evil and persecution and sacrifice. Yet we 'shall be comforted' because the cause for which we have suffered these things will in the end triumph. The gospel will be shown to be true, the promises of God will be fulfilled, evil will be defeated, and we will be rewarded. How then is mourning a positive thing? How is this so?

First, because our mourning leads to salvation.
True repentance always involves grief for sin. The components of repentance are the mind, which confesses; the will, which turns from sin to righteousness; and the emotions, which grieve. This last element is often overlooked, but is vital. You will know from human relationships that interpersonal offenses are only truly resolved when there is sorrow for the offense. If one says, 'I'm sorry,' even, 'I'm sorry and it won't happen again,' and does so in a way that is perfunctory or flippant or superficial, it will not prove to be enough. You may know of cases where it is said, 'she can't just let it go. She keeps bringing it up. She can't seem to forgive or forget.' Why not? Sometimes (not always), but sometimes this happens because he acts like the offense is 'no big deal,' and seeks refuge in lame 'no one is perfect' excuses. He treats it lightly and dismisses it too quickly. Her feelings are not validated. Her wounds are left untreated. What is missing? Her wounds are only healed when there is what has been called 'emotional restitution,' that is, grief on the part of the offender that is proportionate to the grief of the offended. 'I can't believe that I have done that to you,' the repentant husband says. He grieves that he has hurt his wife. Her sorrow makes him weep. He seeks ways to make it up to her. Only then does the victim know that the offender understands the seriousness of what he has done and is truly sorry for having done it. Only then does true forgiveness and reconciliation occur, and with it the peace that accompanies restored relationships. You may have seen this principle illustrated with particular clarity in relation to children. You know when

they say 'I'm sorry' and don't mean it. You can see it in their faces and hear it in their voices. When they are truly sorry for having disappointed and hurt their parents they are broken-hearted, often with tears. Reconciliation, in these circumstances, is sweet indeed. James says,

> Draw near to God and He will draw near to you. Cleanse your hands, you sinners; and purify your hearts, you double-minded. Be miserable, and mourn, and weep; let your laughter be turned into mourning, and your joy to gloom (Jam. 4:8,9).

James says this not because he has a twisted interest in making life unpleasant for others. He says this because in relation to God, deep, heartfelt repentance is the only sure road to forgiveness and reconciliation. You must 'cleanse your hands' and 'purify your hearts' through 'mourning' and 'gloom.' James goes on to say,

> Humble yourselves in the presence of the Lord, and He will exalt you (Jam. 4:10).

In other words, 'humble yourselves' through weeping and mournful repentance and God will restore and even 'exalt' you. Sorrow leads to repentance. Humility leads to reconciliation. This is what Paul tells the Corinthians.

> For the sorrow that is according to the will of God produces a repentance without regret, leading to salvation; but the sorrow of the world produces death. For behold what earnestness this very thing, this godly sorrow, has produced in you: what vindication of yourselves, what indignation, what fear, what longing, what zeal, what avenging of wrong! In everything you demonstrated yourselves to be innocent in the matter (2 Cor. 7:10,11).

See the connections? Godly sorrow leads to 'repentance', which leads to 'salvation.'

So much that we do these days is superficial. I suspect that the reason why so few of us know real joy is because so few of us ever have experienced real grief. Because we've not been humbled, we've not been exalted. Only when we mourn deeply in our hearts are we similarly deeply touched with an awareness of forgiveness and reconciliation. Only when we have been touched by a deep awareness of forgiveness and reconciliation do we experience the peace and the joy that accompany it. Those who mourn are comforted because those who mourn are more profoundly and certainly aware of the reality of a restored relationship with God. I was never so glad to be an American as after I'd spent a year abroad. The grief of homesickness heightened the joy of homecoming to the point of exhilaration. I can remember walking through the L.A. Airport nearly bursting knowing my family was only minutes away. The sorrow of loss leads to the joy of being found. Jesus said, those who are forgiven much love much (Lk. 7:47). Ask yourself, are you still fundamentally an unhappy person? Are you still anxious and unsettled? Have you failed to realize the joy and peace of the Christian life? If so, may it be that you have short-changed the process? Have you mourned that you might be comforted? May it be that you have listened to the prophets of cheap grace who say, 'peace, peace when there is no peace'? Have you listened to too many of the apostles of easy-believism? They seek to heal the wounds of God's people 'slightly,' as Jeremiah said (Jer. 6:14). But a light application of gospel medicine will not heal our spiritual wounds. True comfort is only known by those who truly mourn. You will not have peace, joy, certainty, and assurance until you have deeply grieved your sin and deeply felt forgiveness.

Those who mourn are comforted because they know with greater certainty the fullness of all that the gospel promises. They know that their sins are forgiven. They know that they have eternal life. They know as a result 'the peace that passes comprehension' and the 'joy that is inexpressible and full of glory' (Phil. 4:7; 1 Pet. 1:8). Yes they are comforted. The tears of grief are soothed in knowing they have 'peace with God,' in knowing that there is 'no condemnation' in Christ Jesus (Rom. 5:1; 8:1). They have comfort in knowing that they have been adopted into the family of God, that they are His children and He is their Father, and they can cry out 'Abba! Father!' even as 'His Spirit bears witness with their spirit that they are children of God' (Rom. 8:15,16).

This certainty provides us with a comfort that cannot be shaken. In the world we have tribulation, as Jesus promised, but this peace and joy cannot be taken away. Why? Because our joy is above all 'in the Lord' whom we now know. We 'rejoice in the Lord always' (Phil. 4:4). He never changes. What He gives He does not take back. It is ours now and forever.

Second, our mourning leads to hope.

The 'shall be' to which Jesus is pointing is in the future. Our comfort will only be completely experienced in eternity. Some people are not going to like the sound of that. They will deride such notions as 'pie in the sky,' and so on. Let me say something that you may not want to hear but needs to be said. Most of what we are promised by God in Christ is not received in this world. Ask the martyrs. Ask the heroes of Hebrews 11. We get a taste of redemption in this world, but only a taste. The fullness is not received in this world. Failure to realize this may result in severe disappointment and disillusionment. When things don't go just so, many people crumble. They want to know what went wrong. How have I failed, they wonder? Where is the peace, the joy, the protection, the provision? The answer is, you get only a taste of redemption in this world. Our joy is mingled with sorrow, our peace with fear, our abundance with scarcity, our protection with persecution. Our comfort will only be fully realized in eternity.

Even so, and somewhat ironically, we are comforted now

through the anticipation of that day when we will be in the presence of the Lord where there is the 'fullness of joy' (Ps. 16:11). Our joy is partial now. Then it will be full. Knowing this helps. An example may help. Imagine two men working in exactly the same conditions. Circumstances for both are miserable. Both are grossly underpaid. But one has been promised a $10 million bonus at the end of the year. The other gets no bonus. Do their future hopes affect their respective experiences of present circumstances? Isn't one saying, 'this job is intolerable,' and the other 'I can put up with anything for a bonus like that!'? The promise of future blessing brings comfort out of eternity and into the present. Consequently we can say with the Apostle Paul,

> For I consider that the sufferings of this present
> time are not worthy to be compared with the
> glory that is to be revealed to us (Rom. 8:18).

The certainty of 'glory' then affects my perception of 'the sufferings of this present time.' They are made to be relatively insignificant. They are 'not worthy to be compared' with future glory. With him we come to regard today's suffering as 'momentary, light affliction' (2 Cor. 4:17). Life is short. Eternity is long. This shapes my perspective. Christian people are to have an otherworldly outlook. We set our minds on things above and not on things below. Why? Because that's where Christ is (Col. 3:1-3). Our citizenship is in heaven (Phil. 3:20). Consequently we're not rattled by persecution, or self-denial, or social rejection. We've already learned not to love the world or the things of this world, for 'the world is passing away, and also its lusts.' 'But,' as John says, we know that 'the one who does the will of God abides forever' (1 Jn 2:15-17). We will receive ultimate comfort at this final time of vindication and reward. But we are also comforted *now* in knowing that such a time is coming. Consider the promise of Revelation 21:4.

> He shall wipe away every tear from their eyes;
> and there shall no longer be any death; there shall
> no longer be any mourning, or crying, or pain;
> the first things have passed away. (Rev. 21:4)

Does it not comfort us now to know that we shall receive such comfort then? Doesn't the certainty of future comfort make it all worthwhile now?

Hope has a transforming effect on literally everything. Why are the mourning disciples of Christ blessed and comforted? Because the God who saved them is the God who made and governs the world. Consequently we delight in all that is around us. The creation is the handiwork of our Father. Every tasty morsel of food, every sweet night of sleep, every cool evening breeze, every sunset, every mountain range, every lake or sea is a testimony of His wisdom, power, artistry, and goodness! The people of God delight in this world as a child delights in the strength and wisdom of his father, who seems to know everything and seems able to do anything. We delight in the wonders of this world; in the pleasures of marriage; the comforts of family; the beauty of human artistic expression in music, art, and architecture; and the joys of human community. We enjoy these things more deeply, more profoundly than others because they all manifest the virtues of the God who has made us and saved us.

Perhaps a couple of examples in the context of adversity will help us see more clearly the comfort of the Christian. The Apostle Paul and Silas are beaten with 'many blows,' thrown into prison, and their feet fastened in stocks. This, of course, was a terrible turn of events for them. What a disaster! What suffering! What humiliation! Yet we read,

> But about midnight Paul and Silas were praying
> and singing hymns of praise to God, and the
> prisoners were listening to them (Acts 16:25).

They're singing! Certainly they had suffered enormously. Yet they were comforted. In spite of their circumstances they still knew that their sins were forgiven, that they were adopted children of God, that Jesus was on His throne, that He would return in glory, and He and all His people would be vindicated! So they praised God! So they sang! Blessed are those who mourn.

Or take this other example from earlier in Acts. Peter and the apostles were warned by the Sanhedrin not to preach in the name of Jesus any longer. Then they were flogged, a severe form of beating. How then did they respond? As disciples of Christ they were made to suffer. This may not have seemed to them to be an 'abundant life.' They had been rejected by the leaders of the nation. They had been publicly beaten and humiliated. How did they react?

> So they went on their way from the presence of the Council, rejoicing that they had been considered worthy to suffer shame for His name (Acts 5:41).

Amazing, isn't it? These early Christians understood. Yes they suffered as disciples of Christ. Yes the whips hurt. Yes their hearts ached. Yes they groaned. But they also rejoiced. They had eternity in perspective.

One other example, perhaps my favorite. Paul stands before Festus and King Agrippa. He presents the gospel to them and Agrippa answers.

> In a short time you will persuade me to become a Christian (Acts 26:28b).

Now listen to Paul's response:

> I would to God, that whether in a short or long time, not only you, but also all who hear me this day, might become such as I am, except for these chains (Acts 26:29).

There he is in chains standing before a great king. He is but a poor, lowly prisoner. Yet so conscious is he of the privileges and gifts that he has in Christ that he can say, 'would to God that not only you, but also all who hear me this day, might become such as I am, except for these chains.' This is remarkable. Not, 'O how I suffer,' but, 'O that you might have what I have, and shall have in Christ Jesus!'

This is the joy and comfort of the Christian. The disciple of Christ, with the Apostle Paul, is 'sorrowful yet always rejoicing' (2 Cor. 6:10). His is not the superficial pleasure, the momentary excitement of the worldling, that quickly fades leaving the heart empty and desperate. It is the deep, unyielding, unshakable joy and peace and comfort of Christ's disciples, based on a blessed present, and a certain future.

Lloyd-Jones summarizes in this way,

> As the Christian looks at the world, even as he looks at himself, he is unhappy. He groans in spirit; he knows something of the burden of sin as seen in the world which was felt by the apostles and by the Lord himself. But he is immediately comforted. He knows there is a glory coming; he knows that a day will dawn when Christ will return, and sin will be banished from the earth. There will be 'new heavens and a new earth, wherein dwelleth righteousness.' O blessed hope! 'Blessed are they that mourn: for they shall be comforted' (I,61).

4

Meekness

Is a clear picture of the disciple of Christ beginning to emerge? Christ's people are 'poor in spirit,' deeply aware of their spiritual bankruptcy, their weakness, and unworthiness. They 'mourn' over their spiritual condition, grieving their personal sin as well as the evil and suffering in the world around them. They are 'broken and contrite', looking only to the Lord Jesus Christ for salvation. Now Jesus adds, they are 'gentle,' or 'meek' (*praus*), 'another word for self-effacement,' as Morris notes (98). When asked what were the three most important Christian virtues, the early church father Chrysostom answered, first, humility; second, humility; and third, humility. He was not far from the Sermon on the Mount when he said so. There is a sense in which the first three Beatitudes are variations on the same theme, humility.

The commentators all struggle to find a suitable English word for the Greek original. It is typically translated either 'meekness' or 'gentleness.' New Testament usage helps us to grasp its meaning, as it is coupled with such words and phrases as 'quiet spirit' (1 Pet. 3:4), 'lowly' or 'humble of heart' (Matt. 11:29), 'forbearance' (2 Cor. 10:1), 'humility' (Eph. 4:2), and 'patience' (2 Tim. 2:24,25). J.C. Ryle identifies the meek as 'those who are of a patient and contented spirit. They are willing to put up with little honor here below; they can bear injuries without resentment: they are not ready to take offense' (33). R.T. France says, 'they are those who do not throw their weight about, but rely on God to give them their due' (110). The disciple of Christ, says Morris, 'does not aggressively insist on his own rights' (98).

As is often rightly said, 'meek' should not be confused with 'weak.' The term *praus* was used in antiquity of a domesticated animal, one which perhaps was powerful but submissive, one which 'answers to the reins,' as Barclay put it (I,92). The ancient Greeks and some moderns confuse it with servility, spinelessness, and subservience. This is a mistake. The meek man is not a doormat. He is no Milquetoast. Meekness should not be identified with indolence, flabby thinking, compromise, niceness, or an easy-going manner. The meek person, as the Bible speaks of such, is not meek because he lacks the resources to be anything else, but because he chooses to be. Because he is humble and dependent upon God, he chooses not to assert himself, not to domineer, not to advance personal aims, but is content with lowly service. Meekness, says Stott, 'means 'gentle,' 'humble,' 'considerate,' 'courteous,' and therefore exercising the self-control without which these qualities would be impossible' (42).

The Bible provides two very prominent examples of meekness. It says of Moses, at a time in which his leadership was being challenged by Aaron and Miriam,

> Now the man Moses was very humble, more than
> any man who was on the face of the earth
> (Num. 12:3).

The word 'humble' as translated in the LXX, is the same used in Ps. 37:11 and quoted in Matt. 5:5, *prautes*, meekness. Likewise the greatest man who ever lived said of Himself,

> Come to Me, all who are weary and heavy-laden,
> and I will give you rest. Take My yoke upon you,

and learn from Me, for I am gentle and humble
in heart; and you shall find rest for your souls.
For My yoke is easy, and My load is light
(Matt. 11:28-30).

The word 'gentle' is our word 'meek.'

Several of the commentators (Stott, Carson, Lloyd-Jones)
suggest that the Beatitudes are to be understood progressively.
Why are the people of God meek? Because they are poor in
spirit and mourn their spiritual condition. Of course they are
humble before God, given what they know about themselves.

But the effects of meekness don't merely affect our
relationship with God. They are also seen in our relations with
our fellows. Meekness, the commentators agree, is to be
understood primarily in relation to our fellow men. Meekness
is a gentleness and humility toward others that arises out of a
true understanding of our spiritual condition. Those who
are 'poor in spirit' not only mourn their sins in relation to God,
but are so humiliated by their corruption and worldliness that
they are gentle and humble in relation to others, particularly the
weaknesses of others. Meekness then is an advancement upon
the previous two Beatitudes. It represents a step forward in
spiritual maturity and is far more difficult to acquire. 'We may
acknowledge our own bankruptcy (v 3) and mourn (v 4),' says
Carson. 'But to respond with meekness when others tell us of
our bankruptcy is far harder' (133). Stott says, 'it is comparatively
easy to be honest with ourselves before God and acknowledge
ourselves to be sinners in his sight' (43). But as Lloyd-Jones says,

But how much more difficult it is to allow other
people to say things like that about me! I
instinctively resent it (I.65).

However, to such the promise of God is given – 'they shall
inherit the earth.' Once again Jesus stands the normal human
expectation on end. He cites the promises of Ps. 37:9,11,22,34.

> But the humble will inherit the land, And will
> delight themselves in abundant prosperity
> (Ps. 37:11).

Inheritance of the 'land' is broadened to the whole 'earth' by Jesus (the Hebrew word is the same for both). One might have thought that the humble would get nowhere. The meek will be trampled by the selfishly aggressive and assertive. Often we see that those who get ahead do so by ungodly means, and frequently the meek are their victims. But things are not as they appear. The meek, not the proud, are given a place in God's kingdom. They will inherit all the blessings of time and eternity. They will receive the bounty of both earth and heaven. A great reversal will one day take place. Indeed already the Apostle Paul can say we possess 'all things' (2 Cor. 6:10). 'All things belong to you,' he tells the Corinthians, 'whether ... things present or things to come' (1 Cor. 3:21-22). Why do they inherit the earth? Why this fallen, sin-racked planet? Because there will be a 'new heavens and a new earth, in which righteousness dwells' (2 Pet. 3:13). This earth will be renewed and changed (Matt. 19:28). Indeed heaven and earth will be one (Rev. 21:1ff.). And it will be the righteous lowly, the meek, who will enjoy it all, while those, who through injustice seized the good things in this life, are deprived of it all in the next. Many may gain the world, but lose their soul (Matt. 16:26).

Now that we have a good picture of meekness, we may review its distinguishing marks.

First, the meek are teachable.

Why? Because they have humble views of what they know, what others know, and all there is to be known! James writes,

> Therefore putting aside all filthiness and all that
> remains of wickedness, in humility receive the
> word implanted, which is able to save your souls
> (Jam. 1:21).

60

The word translated 'humility' is our word 'meekness.' Receiving and submitting to the Word requires humility. It takes meekness to have your views changed by the Bible. It takes meekness to have your values reordered. If we think that we already know everything, or at least that our opinions are superior to everyone else's, then we will never learn and never grow. Many of us are people with firm convictions. We believe what we believe strongly! But strong views need not mitigate against learning. The church historians say that Calvin's theology never changed. He got it right the first time. But for most of us, failure to change our minds is a sign of intellectual death. If we've stopped revising, we've stopped thinking. Ask yourself if you have learned anything new in the last fifteen years. Have you had any new insight or fresh understanding in the last decade? If we are truly meek, we will be constantly learning, constantly revising, constantly expanding our knowledge. God's 'compassions' are 'new every morning' said Jeremiah (Lam. 3:23). There is always something heretofore unseen to appreciate in God. Our problem is that our egos can become so wrapped up in our opinions that our views can never change without devastating our whole self-concept. Lloyd-Jones puts it this way:

> we (should) have such a poor opinion of ourselves and our capacities that we are ready to listen to others (70).

Oliver Cromwell said to his divided brethren, 'consider in the bowels of Christ that you might be wrong.' Only those with inflated self-opinions think that they have nothing to learn from others. Even if we are highly educated we should still be ready to listen. Remember the brilliant Abraham Kuyper was converted through the witness of simple peasant women in his parish. In fact, the more we are educated the more meek we ought to become. The overwhelming impression that I had at the end of a year of seminary was how little I knew. The one thing I knew was that I knew nothing. I entered seminary thinking that I knew a lot. I'd studied theology. I'd studied church history. But the exploration of each area of study revealed that I knew next to nothing in relation to all that I needed to know. The more that time passes the more convinced I become that this is always the case. There is a sense in which this awareness ought to stick with us all our lives. The more that we know, the more we realize what we don't know. One of our doctors was telling me about the large book that he read while interning as a general practitioner. Then when he began to specialize he figured that he'd get a thinner book. After all, it would have less material to cover, wouldn't it? Instead, the text covering the narrow area of his specialty was twice the size of his GP text. Essentially the same was true of each sub-specialty as well. This is the way it always is. As we explore new areas of knowledge, we not only learn new information, but we become aware of all that we don't know. Exposure to each of these heretofore unknown worlds of knowledge ought to result in intellectual humility, and with that, teachability.

Those new areas are relatively easy for me to be meek about because I know that I know nothing. However, we each have our areas in which we see ourselves as experts, or at least as knowledgeable in relation to what others know, and our identity is wrapped up in our certainty. Even in these areas the meek one knows his own weakness, foolishness, and ignorance, and so is always ready to learn.

Second, the meek receive correction.

Because they know their own hearts, the meek are ready to hear of their failures and to change. The unmeek, however, are always on the defensive. If someone lovingly identifies a flaw or a fault, the meek receive it and take corrective action. The unmeek recast themselves as martyrs. Consider your own responses to correction. Do you become angry or hurt? Do you think,'they don't understand me. They don't understand my circumstances.' Do you make excuses and explain away your failings? Do you attack the messenger as one who doesn't love you or is out to hurt you? Again Lloyd-Jones says,

> the man who is truly meek is the one who is amazed that God and man can think of him as well as they do and treat him as well as they do (69).

Young people, do you receive your parents' correction joyfully and endeavor to follow their wishes? Employees, do you thankfully receive the correction of your supervisors and endeavor to improve your job performance? Husbands and wives, are you able to receive the complaints of your spouses and improve your respective performances in the home? Or are you defensive? Or do you counter-attack? Or do you pout? The meek are able to receive corrective exhortation because they know that in many areas they fail and are blind to their failure. They know that they need help. They are eager to do better. They are pleased that others care enough to confront.

Third, the meek are gentle with others.
Because they know their own profound flaws, they are tender in dealing with the flaws of others. The critical self-awareness of the meek results in gentleness in handling the failure of others. The proud, however, show no such self-awareness. They live in such a settled state of perfection that they are able to grumble self-righteously and complain about every flawed institution, every imperfect leader, and every defective program. They are unable to look with sympathy and understanding at human frailties. They are unable to see in the weakness of others their own weakness. All they can see is how they would have done things differently or better, given their superior intelligence and moral character. But as Isaiah prophesied of the Messiah, whose words Matthew applied to Jesus,

a battered reed He will not break off, and a smoldering wick He will not put out (Matt. 12:20; cf. Is. 42:3).

The Puritan Richard Sibbes delivered one of the greatest sermons ever preached on this text, drawing out from it the extraordinary tenderness of meek Jesus, who doesn't break the almost broken 'bruised reed' and doesn't quench the barely lit 'smoking flax.' He treats with gentleness the weak of faith, the struggling and discouraged, encouraging, helping, and strengthening them. Looking at the ignorant masses, 'He had compassion on them because they were as sheep not having a shepherd' (Mark 6:14; 8:2; 9:36). Those who are Christ-like do the same. When dealing with opponents, they 'must not be quarrelsome, but be kind to all...patient when wronged,' says Paul,

> with gentleness correcting those who are in opposition, if perhaps God may grant them repentance leading to the knowledge of the truth (2 Tim. 2:25).

When arguing with unbelievers, always be ready, says Peter,

> to make a defense to everyone who asks you to give an account for the hope that is in you, yet with gentleness and reverence (1 Pet. 3:15).

When restoring one who was 'caught in any trespass,' the spiritual ones are not to be self-righteous and condemning, but,

> restore such a one in a spirit of gentleness; each one looking to yourself, lest you too be tempted (Gal. 6:1).

In each of the above verses the word translated 'gentleness' is our word 'meek.' Meek is not weak. It is the quiet, humble strength of those who know their own hearts, and therefore are gentle in their dealings with others. It is the spirit of one who needs compassion and so deals compassionately with others.

Fourth, the meek are modest.
The meek know their weakness, their unworthiness, their inability, and their complete dependence upon God. God has made them. God sustains them. God has saved them. What becomes of pride, of ego when this sinks in? How can we think we're something great in light of our creatureliness? Paul applies the point in this way, humbling the proud Corinthians as he asks,

> For who regards you as superior? And what do you have that you did not receive? But if you did receive it, why do you boast as if you had not received it? (1 Cor. 4:7).

Everything that we have has been given to us by God. How could we boast about our virtues? They are gifts. How could we want to put them on display? This is what the world encourages. If you've got it, flaunt it. This is what the fashion industry thrives on. Broadcast your strengths. Put on display whatever you've got that is better than the rest. Buy the best clothes, the newest car, the biggest house. But are not all these things gifts? How then can we indulge in ostentatious display? How can we imagine ourselves superior to the rest? Your exceptional strength, intelligence, wisdom, or beauty are merely superiorly arranged dust, and God did the arranging! The proud self-made man? He lives a fantasy. His achievements are to be respected. Yet they are not a source of pride. Where exactly would Mr Self-Made be were it not for the moment by moment blessing of God?

To whom does he owe his health, strength, intelligence, beauty, and opportunities? Where would he be if God were to take one or more of these away? What if he had all of his current capabilities but lived in Outer Mongolia? Then what would he have accomplished? The Holy Spirit helps us to see this about ourselves and removes this source of pride. We are but dust.

This is true even with respect to character. Perhaps once you thought that you were something. Once you were self-righteous, you had a high opinion of yourself and of your moral and religious accomplishments. This allowed you to look condescendingly at those you saw as being less moral, or less religious, or less loving, depending on which was your source of pride. But the Spirit helps us to see ourselves as we truly are, and we never forget it. Paul once thought of himself as 'blameless' as measured by the Law. He had a basis for 'confidence in the flesh' (Phil. 3:4-6). But then the Law, particularly the tenth commandment, showed him the true condition of his heart. He came to realize that 'nothing good dwells in me, that is, in my flesh' (Rom. 7:18; cf. 7:7-11).

If nothing good dwells in us naturally, then what do we have to be proud of? Paul saw himself in this light for the rest of his life. 'Worm' theology is disparaged in some circles these days as harmful to healthy self-esteem. Isaac Watts didn't mind singing of 'such a worm as I,' but today we worry about the effect of such sentiments on self-image. Be that as it may, knowing that one is a moral worm has a wonderful effect on Christian character, particularly meekness. It leaves no room for spiritual pride.

Fifth, the meek are ready to serve.
Jesus said,

> If anyone wishes to come after Me, let him deny himself, and take up his cross, and follow Me (Matt. 16:24).

When we became Christians, we lost our lives. We were crucified with Christ (Gal. 2:20). We no longer live for ourselves but for Him (2 Cor. 5:15). Consequently there is no job too menial and no task too lowly that we cannot perform it. We have no turf to protect, no prerogatives to assert. The Holy Spirit gives us joy in serving, whatever the service might be. This outlook marks a watershed in our spiritual development. We must come to the point where we utterly surrender to the will of Christ, where we are willing to do whatever He calls us to do and wherever He calls us to do it. Our service may even involve suffering. We may endure 'the reproach of Christ,' understood as 'abuse suffered for Christ' by P.E. Hughes. If we live for Christ, there is a price to pay. 'If they persecuted me, they'll persecute you,' Jesus said (Jn. 15:20). We're not to be surprised by this (1 Pet. 4:3,4,12). We've been destined for this (1 Thes. 3:3). We could be martyred for Christ. Our name and memory could be disgraced. But the Holy Spirit gives us the capacity to accept this. Our symbol, after all, is a cross! Suffering is our calling. Humbly we submit to this and every form of service. We accept the lowly place without resentment. This is meekness.

In the midst of this the Holy Spirit enables us to see our eternal reward. Consequently, we are able to defer or delay gratification now and meekly endure. People grab for all the toys in this world because 'now' is all that there is for them. This is what drives the acquisitive spirit. This is what is behind our consumeristic, materialistic age. We become pushy and demanding because we want it all now. We demand our own way and our rights, and trample on others in the process. But the Spirit convinces us that 'the meek shall inherit the earth.' Paul writes, 'if we endure, we shall also reign with him' (2 Tim. 2:12). Peter writes,

> Humble yourselves, therefore, under the mighty hand of God, that He may exalt you at the proper time (1 Pet. 5:6).

The way to 'reign' is to 'endure.' The road to exaltation is humility.

I don't have to promote myself and grab all the prizes now. I don't have to step on everyone else as I climb to the top. If I know that a banquet is soon to come, I can forego snacks. I can endure deprivation with calm, with quiet, with strength, and without anger and envy.

Lloyd-Jones points out that the true disciples of Christ are an enigma to the world. The Christian is altogether different from the rest of humanity. He is not proud and self-confident. Rather he is 'poor in spirit.' He is not making an idol of pleasure. Rather he 'mourns.' He is not asserting himself, trampling down others in order to get ahead. Rather he is 'meek.' This baffles and confuses the world. Worldlings scratch their heads in wonder and amusement. 'And if you and I are not, in this primary sense, problems and enigmas to the non-Christians around us,' says Lloyd-Jones, 'then this tells us a great deal about our profession of the Christian faith' (63).

Are you meek? Or does the dragon of pride remain unslain in your heart? May God, the Holy Spirit, grant us the true self-awareness that shall result in humble, gentle, meekness.

5

Hungering and Thirsting
After Righteousness

Blessed are those who hunger and thirst for
righteousness, for they shall be satisfied
(Matt. 5:6).

Thus far Jesus' description of His disciples has been primarily
negative. The Christian is one who understands what his
soul lacks, and so he is 'poor in spirit,' he 'mourns' for his sin,
and he is 'meek.' Because he understands what he is not – he
is not righteous, he is not worthy of heaven, not deserving of
blessing, not capable of pleasing God – he is lowly and humble
before both God and man.

But this is mainly a negative description. What does the
disciple of Christ positively do in response to this negative
self-awareness? Jesus answers: he doesn't sit and sulk. He
doesn't have a pity party. He doesn't give up, saying 'I guess
there is nothing to be done.' He doesn't whine,'I'm a zero.'
He doesn't say,'I'll just lie down here and do nothing.' No in
fact he does just the opposite. In response to his inadequacy
he is fired with zeal to be what he is not, to have what he
lacks. He sees his self-righteousness and pride, and he longs
to be humble. He sees his lust, and he longs to be pure in
heart. He sees his hypocrisy, and he longs to be a man of

integrity. He sees his harsh and condemning spirit, and he longs to be gracious and forgiving. He sees his failure as a father, as a husband, as a friend, and he longs to be fulfilled. He 'hungers and thirsts after righteousness,' and Jesus promises that all who do so 'shall be satisfied.'

Hungering and Thirsting

Hungering and thirsting is a metaphor for intense, focused, even painful longing for something. Think of the person wandering in the desert heat, having gone several days without water. He is obsessed with getting water. He can think of nothing else. He would give all that he has, all of his possessions, if he might just have a single glass of water. The disciple of Christ is one who, because he knows and feels deeply his sinfulness, passionately seeks to be rid of his sin and to replace it with righteousness. This is his first priority. This is his all-consuming desire. He hungers for it. He thirsts for it. He seeks first the kingdom of God (Matt. 6:33). His hunger for righteousness displaces all else. He so loathes his sin; he so abhors the evil that scars his soul that his desire to be rid of it and to be righteous supercedes every other interest, even every other legitimate interest in life. It far overshadows all that once was thought to be critically important. Making a name for oneself, having wealth and things, enjoying pleasure and excitement, being entertained by sports and music all fade into the background. He must have righteousness. He can go without fame and fortune. He can live without things and experiences. But he must have righteousness.

Before we go on to define exactly what Jesus means by 'righteousness,' let's pause to ask, is there anything in your spiritual experience that approaches what Jesus here describes? Have you settled for compartmentalized faith? Have you placed it in a corner of your life, where you can take it out on Sunday morning, dust it off, and then put it back on Sunday afternoon? Is your faith cool and passionless? Is it external and formal? Do you just play at church? If so, do you see that this is not what Jesus had in mind? His disciples are to 'hunger and thirst.' They are passionate about the things of God. They are consumed by them. They long for them. They are their food and drink, their everything, their all. Don't settle for less. Pray that the Lord would now give you such a heart. I remember in college going from being interested in spiritual things to passionately hungering for them. It just happened one week. I don't know how or why it happened. But it did. God opened my eyes and heart. He took me from nominal, safe, guarded belief to radical discipleship. Is it not clear that this is what He wants from us all? He doesn't want us to trifle with the things of God. We are not to pick them up and play with them at our convenience. They are to be our life, our passion. Moreover, we have not begun truly to understand the meaning of life until they are. If our passion, our chief interest, our focus, our priority is sports or self or things or pleasure or anything besides God, then we have misunderstood the meaning of life. We're still lost. To know God at all is to passionately long for Him and His righteousness.

Righteousness

What then does Jesus mean by 'righteousness'? What is this 'righteousness' for which we are to hunger and thirst?

First, He means that we are to hunger and thirst for that God who is righteousness Himself.

He doesn't mean in the first instance that we are to seek after righteousness as an abstract principle. The righteousness we are to seek is God's righteousness, and God's righteousness can only be found in God! R.T. France writes that,

> The meaning here will be that their one desire is
> for a relationship of obedience and trust with God
> (110).

They wish to know God. He writes again,

The ultimate satisfaction of a relationship with God unclouded by disobedience is chiefly in view (118).

This has always been the case with the people of God. Their chief ambition is to know God. They long not just to know about Him, but know Him. The Psalmist writes,

> As the deer pants for the water brooks, So my soul pants for Thee, O God. My soul thirsts for God, for the living God (Ps. 42:1-2a).

Imagine the deer who has just eluded its pursuer. Near exhaustion and dehydration, it 'pants for the water brook'. 'So my soul pants for Thee, O God,' he writes. With all the same intensity and focus the souls of the people of God long to know their God. Again the Psalmist writes,

> O God, Thou art my God; I shall seek Thee earnestly; My soul thirsts for Thee, my flesh yearns for Thee, In a dry and weary land where there is no water (Ps. 63:1).

This Psalm is said to have been written on an occasion when David was in the wilderness/desert, apart from the sanctuary of God and the people of God. He remembers what it was like when he once 'beheld' God in the sanctuary, and saw His 'power' and 'glory' (Ps. 63:2). But now he is in hiding. He looks out on the parched land and sees in it a metaphor of his own soul. Apart from God he is like 'a dry and weary land where there is no water.' So he seeks for God 'earnestly.' He 'thirsts' and 'yearns' for God. He knows that refreshment, satisfaction, fulfillment can only come from God.

Someone will no doubt say that they don't understand. What is so fulfilling about knowing God? He seems so distant, remote. How can He be satisfying? Perhaps we can help our understanding along. Our souls were made for God in much the same way that our souls were made for marriage. This is an imperfect analogy because in this fallen world not every one of us is made for marriage. But if we can overlook the exceptions for a moment, think of that young man who longs to have the hand of a young woman in marriage. Her every movement, her every word is his delight. He contemplates life without her with despair. He pursues her, planning and praying and scheming with inexhaustible energy. What is going on here? Are there not other young women? What's the big deal? There are other fish in the stream, aren't there? Yes but he loves a person, and finds deep meaning and satisfaction in her.

Move to the other end of life. After fifty years of marriage, a man loses the wife of his youth as she succumbs to cancer. Grief overwhelms him. How can he live without her? He experiences a void that he cannot fill. He thinks about her day and night. With her he was content and happy, without her, he feels incomplete, empty, and alone. She was made for him, as it were, and he for her. In both of these cases, happiness is tied to knowing a person. Knowing her means peace, joy, and contentment. Losing her means sorrow upon sorrow. We know what it is to find satisfaction in a person, though certainly this satisfaction is imperfect and incomplete in this world. Jesus is saying that true satisfaction will only be found in knowing the infinite Person, the divine Person, in knowing God. Tragically, our spiritual senses are dead apart from Christ and so we are not aware of our need. We are blind to it. Nevertheless, we were made to know Him. Our fulfillment and satisfaction depend on knowing Him. We will never find them through lesser means. We cannot experience true fulfillment in people or things or pleasures or power. When we encounter Jesus Christ we first begin to realize that He alone can satisfy our souls. The passion to be righteous begins to burn. We must know God. The disciple of Christ is one who is intensely longing for the God who is righteous. Jesus said,

> And this is eternal life, that they may know Thee, the only true God, and Jesus Christ whom Thou hast sent (Jn. 17:3).

Have you yet realized this? Are you still thinking that you'll find fulfillment in this world? This is certainly what our culture tries to tell you. You'll be happy if you just wear these clothes, buy this car, consume this beverage. But it's all a lie. It is deception. The world and its goods cannot satisfy. The world says to you, if you have an itch, scratch it; if you have a desire, fulfill it. Then you'll be satisfied. Then you'll be happy. But it's a lie. Before long the bottle goes dry and the thirst returns. There is always the morning after. But Jesus said to the Samaritan woman at the well and to us,

> Everyone who drinks of this water shall thirst again; but whoever drinks of the water that I shall give him shall never thirst; but the water that I shall give him shall become in him a well of water springing up to eternal life (Jn. 4:13,14).

Again He said,

> I am the bread of life; he who comes to Me shall not hunger, and he who believes in Me shall never thirst (Jn. 6:35).

Do you wish to quench your thirst, your real thirst? Do you wish to satisfy your hunger, the hunger of your soul? When you come to realize that Christ is the living water and the bread of life, then you'll stop toying with religion and begin to hunger and thirst for Christ our righteousness, in whom alone true satisfaction may be found.

Second, Jesus means that we are to hunger and thirst for holiness.

Because the disciples of Christ know that sin separates from God and is abhorred by God, they separate themselves from it and pursue righteousness. J.C. Ryle identifies 'those who hunger and thirst after righteousness' in these words:

> He means those who desire above all things to be entirely conformed to the mind of God (33).

D.A. Carson writes,

> These people hunger and thirst, not only that they may be righteous (ie. that they may wholly do God's will from the heart), but that justice may be done everywhere. All unrighteousness grieves them and makes them homesick for the new heaven and earth – the home of righteousness (2 Pet. 3:13) (134).

Thus this hunger for righteousness is manifest in a desire both to know God and to be like Him. We come to abhor and abominate the things that God abhors and abominates (Rom. 12:9). Christ's disciples are known for their zeal for godliness. They have a passion for obedience. They want nothing more than to be like Christ. It is for this that they hunger and thirst. They wish to be righteous in their thoughts, words, and deeds. They wish to be righteous in their various roles and functions, whether as fathers or mothers, sons or daughters, employers or employees, neighbors or church members or citizens.

How?

How do we do this? You may see that you are lacking this hunger and thirst after God and his righteousness

Primarily this is a matter of the heart, of hungering and thirsting, of passionately longing and desiring. But this internal passion is inevitably manifested in action.

First, we must ruthlessly separate ourselves from sin.
How ruthlessly? In the very chapter which we are now studying,
Jesus, in the context of teaching about lust that leads to adultery,
says,

> And if your right eye makes you stumble, tear it
> out, and throw it from you; for it is better for you
> that one of the parts of your body perish, than
> for your whole body to be thrown into hell. And
> if your right hand makes you stumble, cut it off,
> and throw it from you; for it is better for you that
> one of the parts of your body perish, than for
> your whole body to go into hell (Matt. 5:29,30).

It is difficult to think of how a person could more vividly
illustrate a no-nonsense approach to holiness. Amputate
whatever offends! The Apostle Paul warned the Corinthians
to 'flee immorality' (1 Cor. 6:18). Don't chat with it. Don't
sip coffee with it. Take flight, as did Joseph before us (Gen.
39:7ff.). 'Flee from these things,' Paul says of the love of
money and other sins, 'and pursue righteousness, godliness,
faith, love, perseverance and gentleness. Fight the good fight
of faith...' (1 Tim. 6:11,12). 'Flee youthful lusts,' Paul told
Timothy (2 Tim. 2:22). We must be brutally honest and
thoroughly ruthless about these things. Whatever leads us to
sin, whether it is in a bottle, on a screen, or sitting in the chair
beside me; whether the sin is drunkenness, lust, gossip, self-
righteousness, pride, judgmentalism, or hypocrisy, it must be
eliminated without delay. View it as you would a snake or rat
in your kitchen. Take immediate action! Flee from it or
destroy it. We are to 'abhor what is evil' (Rom. 12:9). That's
right. Abhor it as you would the discovery of a fly in your
glass of water. What is that but material impurity? That's all.
It's just dirt and germs. Yet we view such things with revulsion.
How much worse is spiritual and moral impurity. Loathe sin.
Hate it. Put it to death (Rom. 8:13). Abominate it.

There is a sense in which we are to view these issues in terms of our loyalty to God. Again, we are not dealing with an abstract law, but with a Person. Given what He has done for me in Christ, how could I offend Him? How could I grieve the Holy Spirit? How could I provoke Him? I will do whatever I need to do to live a life that is pleasing to Him. Indeed I will make that my chief ambition in life, that I may be pleasing to God (2 Cor. 5:9). The love of Christ constrains us (2 Cor. 5:14)! He died for us all,

> ...that they who live should no longer live for themselves, but for Him who died and rose again on their behalf (2 Cor. 5:15.

Second, we must zealously pursue righteousness through the means that Christ has given.

We are not only to 'abhor what is evil' but also 'cling to what is good' (Rom. 12:9). We are not only to 'flee' immediately but 'pursue' righteousness (1 Tim. 6:11,12; 2 Tim. 2:22). We are not only to 'put off' all 'anger, wrath, malice, slander, and abusive speech,' but also 'put on the new self' (Col. 3:8-10). This is the pattern in Scripture. Put off and put on! The negative instruction is put off sin. The positive is put on righteousness. I recently read the book *Cry the Beloved Country* by Alan Paton, a powerful, moving novel about South Africa. One point that he makes is that when modernity destroyed the African tribal system, it destroyed a system which, for all its superstition and witchcraft, was a moral system, a system of order and tradition and convention which restrained evil tendencies. Young men and women did not grow up to be criminals and prostitutes when the tribe was strong. The destruction of the tribe by modern culture was inevitable, but it failed to replace the tribe with another system of restraint. It 'put off,' one might say, but failed to 'put on.' Consequently, as Paton sees it, the cities of South Africa, particularly Johannesburg, were flooded with young Africans with nothing to do, and with no moral restraints, bringing with them drunkenness, violence, crime, and destruction. This historical example parallels our own personal sanctification. It is not enough to 'put off' evil. One must also 'put on' righteousness. Those who wish to know Christ and be like Christ passionately pursue the means by which such might be done: worship, fellowship, prayer. faithfulness in public worship.

1. Faithfulness in Public Worship.
Those who hunger and thirst for righteousness gather with the saints for Sunday morning and evening because there they meet with God and the people of God. They are known to say things like,

> How lovely are Thy dwelling places, O Lord of hosts! My soul longed and even yearned for the courts of the Lord; My heart and my flesh sing for joy to the living God. For a day in Thy courts is better than a thousand outside. I would rather stand at the threshold of the house of my God, Than dwell in the tents of wickedness (Ps. 84:1,2a,10).

You don't have to brow beat them into coming to worship. You don't have to beg and plead, cajole, threaten, and promise in order to get them there. They hunger and thirst for worship, because there they meet God, and in meeting God they become more like Him.

They also have a zeal for God's Word. They are known to say such things as

> O how I love Thy law! It is my meditation all the day (Ps. 119:97).

They have been known to liken the Law of God to the desirability of gold and the sweetness of honey (Ps. 19:10).

They meditate upon it day and night. They say,

> Thy word I have treasured in my heart, That I
> may not sin against Thee (Ps. 119:11).

So they hunger for the public reading, and preaching of God's Word. Beyond that they saturate themselves with God's Word throughout the week, ever reading, searching, studying, and meditating upon it. Why? So that they might know God and be like Him.

2. Regular Fellowship with the People of God.

Those who hunger and thirst for righteousness have a zeal for the fellowship of the saints. They are not 'forsaking' the 'assembling together' of the saints, but rather encouraging it because this is where they 'stimulate one another to love and good deeds' (Heb. 10:24,25). Listen to what John says:

> We know that we have passed out of death into
> life, because we love the brethren. He who does
> not love abides in death (1 Jn. 3:14).

This is one of the marks of the true believer. He loves fellow believers and not just those like himself but all believers. He also understands the mutual dependence of believers and their mutual accountability (Rom. 14; 1 Cor. 14). We are members or parts of His body. The disciple of Christ loves the saints. When there is a breakdown in fellowship, He perseveres and makes it work. Why? Because he knows that it is in the church that righteousness is to be pursued. The keys of the kingdom have been given to the church (normally associated with the means of grace) as well as the power of binding and loosing (Matt. 16:19,20; 18:18-20). So he hungers and thirsts for the fellowship of Christian people in Christ's church. His personal devotions are not enough. His private small group Bible study is not enough. He must gather with the whole body of Christ, young and old, rich and poor, those like him and those not like him. He has a zeal for the church, the bride of Christ, for whom Christ shed His blood and whom He nourishes and cherishes (Eph. 5:22ff.). He knows that it is not possible to love Christ and not love Christ's bride. Whom Christ loves he loves.

3. Prayer

Those who hunger and thirst after righteousness have a zeal for prayer. This would include both public and private prayer. Christ's disciples know their weakness. They know that apart from Christ they can do nothing (Jn. 15:5). They need refuge. They need strength (Ps. 46:1). They need daily mercy and help. Without that, they know that they will fail and fall. Consequently they are on their knees before God every day of their life confessing sin, acknowledging guilt, and pleading for forgiveness and grace. Make me a new creation in Christ, they pray. Cause the old sinful ways and habits and priorities and perspectives to pass away and cause all things to become new (2 Cor. 5:17)!

All that! Worship, fellowship, prayer! Separate from sin, pursue righteousness! Someone might be tempted to think that putting off and putting on sounds like an awful lot to do. It sounds rigorous. It may even sound legalistic. But it need not seem so. Think in terms of the material realm. What do you have to do to go to work or school each day, or come to church this morning? There is a whole routine, a discipline that you gladly embrace, that includes putting off bed clothes, bathing, brushing hair and teeth, putting on public clothes, eating, and so on. Some even add to their routine such things as shaving, exercising, and reading the paper. A person might object; the discipline of rising from his bed and changing clothes and fixing breakfast is oppressive to him. He may want to wear his pajamas to church. 'And I don't want to feel like I have to brush my teeth,' he may say. 'I want the freedom to forego that, as well as bathing and eating.' Almost no one talks that way because we have become accustomed to the routine.

Indeed, we feel uncomfortable when we go out without a shower or brushing teeth and hair or eating. It is not oppressive to us, but rather satisfying and pleasurable.

So it is with spiritual disciplines. Initially they may seem complex and overwhelming. First I put off my pajamas, then I take a shower, then I have to put on what? Then do what? And then? And then? But before long it becomes routine, and it cleanses and nourishes the soul. It becomes the most natural thing in the world to attend Sunday services and to have daily private and family devotions. We derive great satisfaction and pleasure from them. We can't bear to miss them.

Satisfied

As we have seen, Jesus promises satisfaction to all who hunger and thirst. They, and they alone, shall be satisfied, a word (*chortazo*) that was used of feeding animals to the point of contentment. They shall be satiated. They shall be fulfilled. The promise is that those who hunger and thirst – not those who trifle and play at religion – but those who hunger and thirst, will be satisfied. Someone might say, 'I've been involved in religion all my life, and I've never experienced the pay-off. I've not found fulfillment or satisfaction. It has always been dry and mostly irrelevant for me.' Perhaps this is because you've tried to find God on a part-time basis. You've kept Him at a distance and limited His place. You've tried to domesticate and tame God and keep Him under control, that is, in a corner. That will never do. Those who are satisfied are those who 'hunger and thirst.' Why? Because they will find righteousness not in themselves, but in Christ. As they pursue the things of God with all their heart they will find the answer to their sin that separates them from God in the cross of Christ. With Him they find righteousness that is given as a gift, an imputed righteousness (Rom. 3:21–24; 4:2–12). With Him they find forgiveness, reconciliation to God, and eternal life. In knowing God they will find that One who alone can fill the void of the human heart, who alone can address our deepest need, who alone can bring satisfaction and fulfillment. With Christ come the 'peace that passes comprehension' and 'the joy that is inexpressible and full of glory' (Phil. 4:7, 1 Peter 1:8).

Beyond this, in hungering and thirsting for practical holiness or Christ-likeness, they find the only life that is worth living. In knowing Christ our hearts are transformed. We are 'born again' (Jn 3:1ff.). We become new creatures in Christ, the old things and old ways 'pass away' and 'all things become new' (2 Cor. 5:21). We have a new life (Gal. 2:20; Rom. 6:4). What life is that? The life conformed to the will of God. The life worth living, the life that satisfies, to the utter amazement of the world, is the life lived in submission to the Law of Christ and to the glory of Christ. It is not to be had 'out there.' It is to be found 'in Him.' And He is to be found only as we abandon ourselves to Him, casting aside all our idols and lusts and pursuing, yea, hungering and thirsting after Him with all our hearts.

6

The Merciful

Ask yourself this question: what is Jesus doing to us in delivering these Beatitudes? What response is He anticipating? It should be clear by now that He is subjecting us to a very thorough process of self-examination. He raises each of these Beatitudes for our consideration, and by doing so implicitly invites us to evaluate ourselves in light of them. He is subjecting us to a test. Now ask yourself, how do I feel about this test? Do I see it as a good thing? As He probes and searches my heart and life, do I regard it positively, or negatively? As Martin Lloyd-Jones points out, my response says a lot about me as a Christian. There may be a temptation to resent it. After all, this test can make us uncomfortable. There may be pain involved. We may convince ourselves that this kind of introspection is morbid or even harmful. But the basic fact is, that since Jesus initiates it, it must be a good thing. It is good for me to ponder whether or not I am poor in spirit, or whether or not I mourn my sins, or whether or not I am meek, or whether or not I hunger and thirst for righteousness. It is good and right for me to weigh my soul against these standards, and good for me to realize my short comings, and good for me to be humbled by the process. As Lloyd-Jones says, 'A man who is truly Christian...never objects to being humbled' (I,96). If I dislike this sort of thing, preferring to move on and talk about 'positive' things or politics or sports or something else, then I need to remember that it is not the preacher but Jesus who places this mirror before our eyes and requires that we look into it. This is what our divided, self-deceived hearts need, and the Great Physician knows it (Jer. 17:9). It is the road to spiritual maturity, to sanctification, to Christ-likeness.

Ask yourself a second question. About what is Jesus most concerned? It is indisputably clear, is it not, that His central focus is the condition of our hearts? His emphasis is upon attitude not actions, on character and disposition rather than activity. 'Being is more important than doing, attitude is more significant than action,' notes Lloyd-Jones (I,96). Jesus will say a great deal about what a Christian does and does not do later in the Sermon. But He gives this emphasis at the outset in order to make clear that being a Christian is not primarily a matter of doing certain things. I do not become a Christian by doing thus and so. Being a Christian is primarily a matter of the heart. This is why we must be changed from within, by being 'born again' as Jesus put it (Jn. 3:1ff.). If I find that my heart is not as Jesus describes, and I have come to the place that I recognize this to be true, then praise God because salvation is right at the door. Now I am ready to confess my sin and plead for a changed heart, in other words, plead that God will do that which only He can do, saving me and changing me.

With grateful and willing hearts we come to the fifth of the Beatitudes:

> Blessed are the merciful, for they shall receive mercy (Matt. 5:7).

We may notice a distinction here. The first four Beatitudes seem to be primarily (though not entirely – see sermon on meekness) concerned with our relationship to God. In relation to our great and holy God, we are poor in spirit, acknowledging our spiritual poverty; we mourn the cause of our spiritual poverty that is sin, especially as it is present in our own hearts; we are meek in relation to God and man, our behavior being conditioned by our awareness of our true spiritual condition; and we hunger and thirst after righteousness, longing to be other, better than we now are, and finding forgiveness and acceptance through the imputed righteousness of Christ. But now there is a shift in focus from God to man. Now Jesus is concerned primarily with the effects or consequences of the first four Beatitudes on our conduct toward others. Because the traits of the first three Beatitudes are characteristic of us, we conduct ourselves toward others in these ways – we are merciful, we are pure in heart, we are peacemakers, and we rejoice when persecuted. The first of these is our concern today.

Meaning

Of what and of whom is Jesus speaking when He identifies the 'merciful' as 'blessed'? Stott defines 'mercy' as compassion for people in need. The merciful are those who are habitually merciful, whose lives are characterized by mercy. He 'means those whose bent is to show mercy, not those who engage in planned and occasional merciful impulse,' says Morris (110). 'He means those who are full of compassion toward others,' says J.C. Ryle (33). Most of the commentators draw a distinction between grace, which deals with sin itself, providing pardon from guilt, and mercy, which deals with the results or consequences of sin. Or to put it another way, grace is concerned with forgiveness of sin, while mercy is concerned with relief from the pain, alienation, misery, and distress that is caused by sin.

In recent months we have begun reading as a family the *Trailblazer* books, a series of adventure stories introducing young readers to heroic Christians of the past. We have encountered Mary Slessor, a Scottish Presbyterian missionary who worked in the most primitive circumstances in what is now southern Nigeria, battling witchcraft, twin-murder, polygamy, slavery, and even cannibalism. We have read of Gladys Aylward's courageous work among the Chinese during the tumultuous 1930s and 40s, ministering to coolies and mule-train drivers, helping to end the practice of foot-binding, and relieving suffering wherever she encountered it even in the midst of Japanese attacks. We have read of the Quaker Elizabeth Fry's work for prison reform in Great Britain, laboring ceaselessly to improve the lives of the female inmates. In each case these women were motivated by mercy. Slessor adopted at least seven children herself and Aylward five! They saw people in need, both physically and spiritually, and gave their lives to the relief of their distress.

It is this quality of helpful compassion, of sympathetic interest and activity that Jesus commends and identifies as 'blessed.' We live in a fallen world and are often surrounded by the consequences of the fall. Because there is sin in the world, we encounter poverty. The merciful will try to secure material provision for the poor. We will encounter children who are orphaned. The merciful will find families for them. We will encounter unwanted pregnancies. The merciful will build homes for unwed mothers. We will encounter ignorance. The merciful will provide schools. We will encounter crippled or handicapped bodies. The merciful will care and help. We will encounter sickness. The merciful will seek to heal. We will encounter war. The merciful will soothe the wounds. We will encounter crime. The merciful will provide protection. And of course we will encounter the spiritually lost. The merciful will bring to them the gospel. The world may turn away in contempt or disgust from the weak and needy. The disciples of Christ respond with compassionate and sympathetic help.

We should take pains to distinguish the real virtue of mercy from what it is not. Jesus is not commending an easy-going personality. Some of us have a natural disposition that tends to accept and deal with people where we find them. Live and let live they say. As we've seen, Jesus never commends a given personality type, though some personalities do have common grace advantages in dealing with certain sins.

Similarly, He is not advocating the suspension of moral judgments. He is not commending the acceptance of sin, smiling at law-breaking, winking at perversion. Some have made the mistake of identifying mercy with the condoning of whatever moral degradation comes our way. The merciful are never judgmental or critical, but kindly accepting one and all, they say. There is a foolproof argument against this view – God Himself is merciful yet He never indulges sin. Zacharias spoke of 'the tender mercy of our God' (Lk. 1:78). He is 'full of compassion and is merciful' (Jam. 5:11). He is 'rich in mercy' (Eph. 2:4). Jesus is 'a merciful and faithful high priest' (Heb. 2:17). Yet God never compromises truth and justice in the name of mercy. God shows mercy in Christ, but only at the cost of the cross, never in the process compromising His Law. He is 'compassionate and gracious, slow to anger, and abounding in loving-kindness and truth,' yet 'He will by no means clear the guilty' (Ex. 34:7). 'Do not be deceived,' Paul warns, 'God is not mocked; for whatsoever a man soweth, that shall he also reap' (Gal. 6:7). God is both 'just and justifier,' as truth and mercy 'kiss' in Christ (Rom. 3:26; Ps. 85:10). Mercy does not condone sin. In fact this is what makes mercy an even stronger quality than it otherwise would be. While Christian mercy condemns sins, it looks with sympathy and kindness at those suffering from its consequences.

The Good Samaritan, for example, sees a man lying alongside the road, beaten and robbed. He doesn't know why it has happened or how. He doesn't know if he is a good or bad man. While others pass by the other way, he has mercy on the man and helps him, extending personal care himself and providing for future care through financial provision. 'Go and do the same,' Jesus tells us (Lk. 10:30-37).

Mercy then would not mean leaving the murderer's crime unpunished. That would compromise justice. Mercy rather would provide sympathetic help for the murderer and his family in the midst of his punishment. On the one hand, the world might so despise the criminal so as to completely wash its hands of him, and want nothing to do with him. On the other hand some bleeding hearts might wish to end all punishment for the criminal in order to let him go free, leaving no consequences for his crime at all. The Christian balance is to recognize the demands of justice – those who break the law must receive punishment that fits the crime. Where it doesn't fit the crime, if the punishment is disproportionally severe relative to the offense, then like Elizabeth Fry we should seek to change the law. For example, pickpockets should not be hanged. Petty thieves should not have their children taken from them and be deported. But within the context of just laws, mercy may be extended to give aid and comfort to those suffering the consequences of their wrongdoing. The demands of mercy, of course, go far beyond the issues of social justice. They also reach us at home, in our relationships with one another, in dealing with those who hurt and disappoint us. The disciples of Christ respond to interpersonal conflicts with mercy. Again this is not to say that there are not consequences. But we are to be quick to forgive and restore those who have offended us. We are even to love our enemies (Matt. 5:43,44; 6:15).

Barriers to Mercy

Do you wish to be this kind of person? God can make us such. But there are several barriers that must be overcome for a person to show mercy of this sort.

The first barrier to overcome is self-centeredness.

There are times when we are so self-centered and self-absorbed that we are unable to enter into and understand the suffering of others. Those who are merciful weep with those who weep (Rom. 12:15). They are able to transcend their own favorable circumstances and experience the pain, the sorrow, the misery, the suffering of others, and are motivated to relieve it. Many, however, are not able to break out of their

88

own little world and look beyond their pleasant circumstances. They've never been seriously ill, so they have no sympathy for those who are. They've never been poor, so they have no mercy for those who are. James Jarvis, one of the main characters in *Cry the Beloved Country*, is a rich white man who was a hard-working, decent, moral man who just never noticed the poverty of the Africans all around him. He didn't oppress them. He wasn't hateful. But until his own son was killed, he just never noticed. This is how we can be. We can't see the suffering of those who are around us. When Jesus encountered the sick he was 'moved with compassion' and healed them (Mark 1:41). May God give us the grace to look beyond ourselves, and show mercy to those in need.

The second barrier to overcome is self-pity.

The first problem was one of emotional distance from suffering. This problem is one of preoccupation with one's own suffering. One sees the pain, the sorrow, the heartache, the loneliness of others, whoever they are, and always considers one's own circumstances as worse. The self-pitying say,'I should have it so bad! Look at the sympathy they get! Look at the family support they have! Look at the house! Look at the income! Look at the trips they go on! Look at the clothes! I'm sorry, lots of folks are worse off than they are. I've never had half the things and emotional support that they have.' This outlook makes sympathy toward others, and therefore mercy with respect to their suffering impossible. Because the grass is always greener elsewhere, one can pity no one, only oneself. Such come to see everyone else as moaners and cry babies, whereas no one has it as tough as they do. From such, there will be no mercy.

The right outlook, it seems to me, is to realize that both the circumstances and capacities of others are largely hidden. We don't know what goes into the sorrow of a given person. When I was inclined to being disdainful of what I saw as the self-inflicted pain of the wealthy on Granada Boulevard of

Coral Gables, Florida, my future mother-in-law taught me that there was 'a broken heart behind every door.' One may be materially well-off and yet suffering agonizing emotional or spiritual pain. How are we to respond? With mercy. We only know about what we see, the proverbial tip of the iceberg, while 90 per cent of it lies hidden. Certainly we have our own troubles. But we should not be so self-consumed that we are unable to sympathize with the pain of others.

A third barrier to overcome is pride.

We see a person in pain and we assume that they deserve it. Sometimes we are tempted to play God and try to connect their suffering to specific sin and say they suffer because they did that evil thing. This is exceedingly difficult to do in this world, as Job would have us know. At other times we see an obvious connection between sin and consequences and say, 'I'd never do that,' and are disdainful of those who do. 'He had it coming,' we say. We feel morally superior. We harshly condemn the fallen. We are incapable of mercy because our hearts are filled with contempt for the sinner and his sin. The pregnant teenager, the drunken driver, the addicted drug user, the convicted embezzler all elicit our contempt. 'They brought it on themselves,' we say. Such thinking rules out mercy.

The right response, it seems to me, is to realize that it could be me. I might have done that. I might be guilty of that. 'There but for the grace of God go I.' The meek, as we have seen, are humble, and humility leaves room for mercy. I am able to project myself into those shoes, in that trouble, suffering those consequences, and so sympathize and show mercy toward those who are enduring trials. I know that I am no better than they.

The fourth barrier to overcome is selfishness.

We must now distinguish self-centeredness (our first barrier) from selfishness. Sometimes the self-centered are generous. They just always view life from their own narrow frame of reference. But the selfish worry about expense. They want to keep all that they have for themselves. It is costly to show mercy. It costs a great deal in terms of time, money, and energy. A person might say, 'My plate is full,' and as a consequence refuse to extend help. Now it needs to be said that sometimes our plate truly is full. Sometimes we are at our capacity. Sometimes we are pushed to our absolute limit. But is this always the case? Aren't there occasions when we should put aside non-essentials and be willing to help? May God free us from the temptation to selfishly cling to the resources that He has made available to us.

Jesus saw the multitudes as 'sheep without a shepherd,' and so did what? Ridiculed them for their ignorance? Mocked them for their lack of spiritual insight? After all, they should have known better. No, 'He felt compassion for them,' we're told (Mark 6:34). We ought to look at the lost world around us with all its ignorance, rebellion, and depravity with compassion. The multitudes are blind. They are lost. It is so pathetic. Have mercy on them. Pity the thief. Pity the prostitute. Pity the drug dealer. Pity the pornographer. Pity the sophisticated, educated humanist too. He's just as lost. If we pity them we'll be able to minister to them. If not, I fear we'll only regard them as hopeless non-persons, unworthy of our consideration. Pity and pray for, and reach out to, and have mercy on our inner-city gangs, our unemployed youths, our babies having babies, our crime-infested neighborhoods. Pity and pray for, and reach out to our wealthy but equally lost friends in the nicer neighborhoods as well.

The merciful, Jesus says, are 'blessed.' It may not seem so. Calvin's comments are to the point.

> Here there is a paradox set against human judgment. The world reckons those are blessed who are free of outside troubles to attend to their own peace, but Christ here says they are blessed who are not only prepared to put up with their own troubles but also take on other peoples', to help them in distress, freely to join them in their

time of trial, and, as it were, to get right assistance
(I, 171).

The merciful are getting involved, taking on the troubles of others in addition to their own troubles. Yet they are blessed in this. God promises blessing. 'They shall receive mercy,' He says.

Receiving Mercy

This principle of giving and receiving is often repeated in Jesus' ministry. He says a little bit later in the Sermon on the Mount,

> For if you forgive men for their transgressions, your heavenly Father will also forgive you. But if you do not forgive men, then your Father will not forgive your transgressions (Matt. 6:14-15).

He also tells the parable of the unforgiving steward, who is forgiven a vast debt, but then won't forgive a small debt. His lord asks him,

> Should you not also have had mercy on your fellow slave, even as I had mercy on you? (Matt. 18:33).

Jesus warns,

> So shall My heavenly Father also do to you, if each of you does not forgive his brother from your heart (Matt. 18:35).

Forgiveness and mercy are not merited by our acts of the same. But while they are not the *cause* of such, they are the *occasion*. The point is that those who have received mercy without exception extend mercy. Knowing what they deserve (condemnation) and realizing what they got (mercy), they gladly extend the same to others. Those who cannot and will not forgive are graceless. Those who cannot and will not show mercy have not known mercy. Those who harbor resentments, who grow bitter, who condemn and hate others while congratulating themselves, cannot but be those who have never known the mercy of God.

God is mindful that we are but dust (Ps. 103:14). So also should we be mindful of the weakness of others. Jesus wept over sinful and rebellious Jerusalem. So also should we weep over our lost city and nation. As we show mercy, God is pleased, and we grow ever more confident that on that final day, He will show mercy to us.

7

Pure in Heart

Blessed are the pure in heart, for they shall see
God   (Matt. 5:8).

'How this gospel finds us out,' remarks Martin Lloyd-Jones.
It is constantly poking and prodding, examining this aspect
of our lives and then that. Jesus asks of our spiritual condition
– are we poor in spirit? Do we mourn our sins? Do we know,
in other words, of our spiritual deprivations? Are we meek
and humble as a result of this awareness? Do we long to be
different? Do we hunger and thirst after righteousness? Have
we found satisfaction in righteousness?   Have we been
fulfilled?   Then he comes back at us again in terms of
consequences. If we have been filled, if we have inherited
the kingdom of heaven, can this be seen in our conduct? Are
we merciful? Are we pure in heart? Are we peacemakers?
Then He examines the outcome – are we persecuted for
righteousness' sake? Why? Why not?

   A true disciple of Christ will be characterized by purity of
heart. Such, He says, are blessed. Such, He says,'shall see
God.'

Meaning
Who does Jesus mean by the'pure in heart'?   The
commentators elaborate in two senses.

First, He means those who are inwardly morally pure.

The word 'pure' is the word (*katharos*) from which we derive our English word catharsis, meaning emotional cleansing or release. It was used in antiquity of cleaning clothes or other objects, and of purging an army of malcontents and cowards. The 'heart' indicates not merely the seat of the emotions, as it does in our culture. Rather 'it stands for the whole of our inner state, thought and will as well as emotions,' says Morris (100). The heart for Jesus' listeners was the center of the rational, emotional, and volitional elements of the human personality. Thus Jesus is requiring 'purity at the very center of our being.' Again Morris says, 'to be pure in heart is to be pure throughout' (100).

We may contrast being pure in heart with a mere external purity, even as material poverty might be contrasted with being 'poor in spirit' or spiritually poor. 'He means those who do not aim merely at outward correctness, but at inward holiness,' says J.C. Ryle (33). Carson understands Jesus to mean 'inward moral purity as opposed to merely external piety or ceremonial cleanliness' (134). To be pure in heart is to be pure spiritually, internally, truly. This is characteristic of those who are disciples of Christ, who are blessed.

'Search me, O God,' the Psalmist prays (Ps. 139:1). Is my life characterized by moral purity? Am I living a clean, pure, holy life? Or am I allowing corruption into my life one small step at a time? Have I begun to tolerate dishonesty? Or pride? Or lust? Or coveteousness? Am I indulging lies, even if they're only white lies? Am I indulging theft, even if its only petty theft? Am I indulging 'innocent' flirtations, 'harmless' gossip, or 'soft' pornography? The Scripture attacks sin in its seed. It cautions us to guard our speech from 'unwholesome words,' from silliness and 'coarse jesting' (Eph. 4:28–5:1ff.). It cautions us to dress 'modestly and discreetly,' not in ways that are sensual or provocative. Am I living according to the Scripture? Am I keeping the Ten Commandments? Am I obeying the law of love? What would my family say? What would the people at work say? What would my neighbors say? We are called to be holy even as God is holy (1 Pet. 1:16). Most importantly, what would God say?

Notice, Jesus doesn't say 'blessed are the pure.' One might be able to claim a pure record, as Paul could (Phil. 3:4 ff.). No, His concern is more comprehensive than that. He says blessed are the pure *in heart*. His concern is with internal, heart purity, not external show. The complaint of the prophets going back to Moses was that God's people lacked the internal, spiritual circumcision that corresponds to external, physical circumcision. 'Circumcise then your heart,' He told them (Dt. 10:16; cf 30:6). God warned through Jeremiah,

> Circumcise yourselves to the Lord and remove the foreskins of your heart, men of Judah and inhabitants of Jerusalem... (Jer. 4:4a; cf 9:25,26).

God was not pleased with the right and proper moral and ceremonial form without heart obedience. He asked through Isaiah,

> 'What are your multiplied sacrifices to Me?' says the Lord. 'I have had enough of burnt offerings of rams, and the fat of fed cattle. And I take no pleasure in the blood of bulls, lambs, or goats.' (Is.1:11).

What He wanted was internal purity:

> Wash yourselves, make yourselves clean; remove the evil of your deeds from My sight. Cease to do evil, learn to do good; seek justice, reprove the ruthless; defend the orphan, plead for the widow (Is. 1:16,17).

Similarly Jesus rebuked the Pharisees, calling them 'whitewashed tombs.' They were ceremonially correct. They washed 'the outside of the cup and of the dish.' But the problem was that 'inside they are full of robbery and self-indulgence' (Matt. 23:25-27). Again He said,

> Even so you too outwardly appear righteous to men, but inwardly you are full of hypocrisy and lawlessness (Matt. 23:28).

All of which is to say, it is possible to play church and yet be a total hypocrite. One can be present at services Sunday morning and Sunday night and Sunday school. One can attend circles and special services. One can baptize one's children and receive the Lord's Supper. One can tithe one's income and keep a very strict Sabbath. One can conduct daily family worship and catechize one's household. In other words, one can do all the things externally that one is supposed to do and yet be utterly unconverted.

Not only can it be the case, but often it is the case. Churches all over this land are filled with people who pretend to be Christians who do all the right things but who are self-deceived. Go to church though they may, their hearts are filled with anger, hate, bitterness, envy, covetousness, pride, lust, bigotry, judgmentalism, and so on. Note these are all sins of the heart. They can go undetected for a time. But God knows the heart (1 Sam. 16:7). He is not pleased with mere external correctness. Our hearts must be right as well. Paul's critique of the Judaism of his day was similar to that of Jesus.

> For he is not a Jew who is one outwardly; neither is circumcision that which is outward in the flesh. But he is a Jew who is one inwardly; and circumcision is that which is of the heart, by the Spirit, not by the letter; and his praise is not from men, but from God (Rom. 2:28,29).

Ask yourself, have you settled for an external, outward form of Christianity? Is your baptism a baptism of the flesh only or of the Spirit? Are you resting on external religious ceremonies and observances and neglecting the heart? Particularly vulnerable are those who have been reared in the church, but have never been 'born again' (Jn. 3:1 ff.). Are you trusting in forms and rituals? Child of the church, has your heart been changed? Are you a 'new creation' (2 Cor. 5:17)? If we are to see God, we must be pure in the depths of our souls. Jesus means nothing less.

Second, He means those who are sincere.

In addition to clean, 'pure' should be understood as meaning unmixed, or undivided. The pure in heart are those whose hearts are not divided by conflicting concerns. R.T. France argues that the phrase indicates not just moral purity, but 'it denotes one who loves God with all his heart (Dt 6:5), with an undivided loyalty' (110). According to Stott, 'the primary reference is to sincerity' (49). The one who is pure in heart then is one who is free from falsehood, who is utterly sincere and transparent. He is characterized by pure thoughts and motives. He is without deceit, hypocrisy, or guile. He is not pretending to be something he is not. He is not play-acting. He does not construct a false world of make-believe and deceit. The disciple of Christ is straightforward, honest, and lives with integrity.

Is my heart undivided? Is it pure in the sense of being unmixed, undiluted, uncorrupted, in the way that we might speak of pure sugar or pure water? For the disciple of Christ, a pure heart means undivided loyalty, an undiluted commitment, and unmixed motives. Our heart, in other words, belongs entirely to the Lord. Is my profession of Christ sincere? Or is it superficial and hypocritical? Is it a matter of convenience? Am I committed to Christ until something else comes along that for that moment pleases me more? Am I pretending to be something I am not? Is my Christian commitment a facade, or worse, a farce? Who might I be trying to kid?

Once again I am afraid that the church is troubled by this sort of confusion. Some seem to derive a form of social satisfaction from the appearance of Christian commitment. They may even believe that they are truly committed to Christ. But it doesn't take long to discover that they love the world too, and more. Thus they dare not buck the world, or offend the world. Their loyalties are divided. Their hearts are not pure, but mixed with self-interest and pride. They will, at all costs, guard their wealth and reputations. They are not pure, but polluted. They are not pure, but corrupted. They are, in a word, hypocrites, pretending through external show to be something that they know they are not internally.

Ask yourself, is my love of God pure? Does He have my whole heart? Does He have my absolute allegiance? Or is my heart divided? Our hearts must be pure, singular, uncorrupted. Do you love wealth more? Or sports? Or power? Or pleasure? Only the pure will see God. No one else shall.

Promise

Let us now examine the blessing that Jesus promises will accompany purity of heart.

First, we note that purity is a good thing.

In one sense purity is its own reward. It is good to be pure. What we easily understand in the physical realm is also true in the spiritual and moral. We appreciate clean air, don't we? How about clean plates in a restaurant? Moral purity is just as important and just as beautiful as purity in our physical environment. Persons who love with pure motives, not courting advantage, and persons who help with absolute sincerity, not looking for gain, are wonderful to meet and know, aren't they? The faithful husband, the chaste teenager, the honest politician, the reliable businessman – these are good and highly desirable models of purity. We ought to aspire to purity in thoughts, words, and actions. Such purity results in stable homes, safe neighborhoods, decency in culture, honest governments, reliable businesses, and effective schools.

In addition, we can speak of the psychological or emotional benefits of purity. What price tag would you put on a clear conscience? The swindler, the shady dealer, the hypocrite all look in the mirror each day and see a fraud. Granted some people sear their consciences so they are no longer troubled by such things. But many others turn in their beds at night knowing that their hands have been fouled by cheating and lying. 'The fear of the Lord leads to life,' says the Proverbs, 'so that one may sleep satisfied, untouched by evil' (19:23).

What is the value of a clear conscience toward God? How many live life with the nagging, even tormenting sense that they are not right with the God before whom they will one day stand? To be able to stand before God knowing that one has lived not perfectly but with sincerity and integrity is invaluable.

The world may scoff at 'Goody-two-shoes' but the results are desired by all, and there is no shortcut to those benefits. Personal and universal purity is the only way. Where we see corruption we must seek to rid our hearts of it.

Second, purity, like righteousness, is to be vigorously pursued.

We are to love 'from a pure heart' (1 Tim. 1:5). We are to serve God with a 'clear (same word) conscience' (2 Tim. 1:3). We are to,

> flee from youthful lusts, and pursue righteousness,
> faith, love and peace, with those who call on the
> Lord from a pure heart (2 Tim. 2:22).

Do you see who does the fleeing and pursuing? You do! Flee lust! Pursue righteousness! We are to 'purify' our 'souls' so that we might love one another sincerely and fervently 'from the heart' (1 Pet. 1:22). The Apostle Paul says,

> Let us cleanse ourselves from all defilement of flesh and spirit, perfecting holiness in the fear of God (2 Cor. 7:1).

We and no one else are called to 'cleanse ourselves' (same root word) and perfect holiness. We are to care about purity, pray for it, seek it, and not rest until we realize it in our attitudes and conduct.

Third, purity is rewarded.

What does Jesus promise? That we shall 'see God.' Think of the privilege. The pure in heart will see God. Consider the great expense in time, energy, and money that people are willing to incur to see beautiful things, places, and people. God is infinitely more beautiful to behold than even the most perfectly proportioned and exquisitely beautiful objects and persons that ever have been. The Psalmist can consider no greater privilege than to enjoy God's beauty. He says,

> One thing I have asked from the Lord, that I shall seek: That I may dwell in the house of the Lord all the days of my life, To behold the beauty of the Lord, And to meditate in His temple (Ps. 27:4).

What is the 'one thing' that he asks for? That he might dwell in God's house not as an end in itself, but so that he might 'behold the beauty of the Lord.' Again he says,

> How lovely are Thy dwelling places, O Lord of hosts! My soul longed and even yearned for the courts of the Lord; My heart and my flesh sing for joy to the living God (Ps. 84:1,2).

God's 'dwelling places' are 'lovely' because God is there! Similarly, consider what a privilege it would be to have an audience with the wisest and most eloquent person who ever has lived. Can you remember hearing brilliant oratory that awed and fascinated and left you longing for more? Think of Lincoln's Gettysburg Address or Churchill's stunning oratory during the dark days just prior to and during World War II. Or think of your reactions when you have read a truly great book. You long to meet the author, don't you? Yet God is infinitely more wise and eloquent than any person. His wisdom will amaze us eternally. What about the appeal of a person who has extraordinary charm. Think how you love to be in their presence, even if you are silent in their presence. God's mere presence will thrill our souls.

> In Thy presence is fulness of joy; In Thy right
> hand there are pleasures forever (Ps. 16:11).

Where will the Psalmist find 'the fullness of joy' and 'pleasures forevermore'? 'In Thy presence,' he says. There is no greater promise than this – to see God. To see God is to see, to experience, to know the most beautiful, the most wonderful, the most desirable One in all of creation.

When may I see him, you ask? It begins right now. In Christ we know God (Jn. 17:3). We see Him 'with the eyes of faith' (Carson, 135). By faith, like Moses, we see 'Him who is unseen' (Heb. 11:27). Yet a full view of God only comes later. Now we see only His back (Ex. 33:23). Now we get but a taste (Ps. 34:8). Now we look through a glass darkly (1 Cor. 13:12). We can bear to see no more. That future vision is 'too wonderful to be fully experienced in this life,' says Morris (100). Then in order to see Him we shall be made like Him (1 Jn. 3:1-3). Then we shall know 'fully,' just as we have been 'fully known' (1 Cor. 13:12).

Fourth, purity is actual.

Do you wish to see God? Then God must purify your heart. You must be changed. The writer to the Hebrews says that we are to pursue that holiness 'without which no one will see the Lord' (Heb. 12:14). 'Who may ascend into the hill of the Lord? Who may stand in His holy place?' The Psalmist answers,

> He who has clean hands and a pure heart, who has not lifted up his soul to falsehood, And has not sworn deceitfully (Ps. 24:3-4).

Again he asks,

> O Lord, who may abide in Thy tent? Who may dwell on Thy holy hill? He who walks with integrity, and works righteousness, and speaks truth in his heart. He does not slander with his tongue, nor does evil to his neighbor, nor takes up a reproach against his friend (Ps. 15:1-3).

Our God not only saves us but also makes us pure. He not only justifies us but also sanctifies us. To see God, one must be made holy. He not only imputes righteousness to us but makes us righteous. Light and darkness cannot be mixed (2 Cor. 6:14). Do you wish to be near to God? James tells us,

> Draw near to God and He will draw near to you. Cleanse your hands, you sinners; and purify your hearts, you double-minded (Jam. 4:8).

Nearness to God is related directly to cleansing the hands and purifying the heart. This is the teaching of this Beatitude. Listen again to the Apostle Paul:

> Or do you not know that the unrighteous shall not inherit the kingdom of God? Do not be

> deceived; neither fornicators, nor idolaters, nor adulterers, nor effeminate, nor homosexuals, nor thieves, nor the covetous, nor drunkards, nor revilers, nor swindlers, shall inherit the kingdom of God. And such were some of you; but you were washed, but you were sanctified, but you were justified in the name of the Lord Jesus Christ, and in the Spirit of our God (1 Cor. 6:9-11).

Only those who have been 'washed' and 'sanctified' as well as 'justified' from the sins listed will inherit the kingdom of God. Similarly, following a long list of sins in Galatians 5:19-21 Paul warns that those who were turning Christian freedom into an 'opportunity for the flesh,' that those who 'practice' such sins, *'shall not inherit the kingdom of God'* (Galatians 5:13, 21). Clearly the expectation is that there will be actual separation from sinful practice. God's people will be holy because He is holy (1 Pet. 1:16).

These kinds of things can be said and indeed are said repeatedly throughout the Bible without compromising the graciousness of the gospel because justification and sanctification always go together. Those whom God saves He also transforms and changes. They become 'new creatures' in Christ. They are born again, with new hearts, and with the gift of the Holy Spirit (2 Cor. 5:17; Jn. 3:1ff.). What then is the condition of your heart? Is it pure? In Christ it is, though in this world not completely. We are pure though that purity is not perfected until the consummation. Yet we can speak meaningfully of the difference between being imperfectly pure as opposed to impure. Jesus replaces our old filthy hearts and gives us new ones. He cleanses and purifies us internally and spiritually.

The 'old self' is crucified, the 'body of sin' is 'done away,' and we are raised up in 'newness of life' (Rom. 6:4-6). But the dregs of sin remain. Life thereafter for the Christian is a process of putting to death the remnants of sin that are within. 'You will live,' says the Apostle Paul, 'if by the Spirit you are putting to death the deeds of the body' (Rom. 8:13). Note, this is done 'by the Spirit.' Note as well that life, spiritual and eternal, depends on it. Only Christ can empower and enable us to 'crucify the flesh with its passions and desires' (Gal. 5:24; cf. Col. 3:5). But the point is that it is done, we are made righteous, just, clean, and pure, not merely judicially, but actually, truly, really in practice and experience. This may sound unnerving to some Christians, but primarily the 'actual' cleansing of the believer should be seen as a promise rather than a warning. Though it is a struggle and fight to grow in Christ-likeness, to bear the fruit of the Spirit, and to become holy, it will happen.

Again we ask, do you wish to see God? Then turn to Jesus, who alone can make you fit for heaven. Turn to Jesus and be ushered into the presence of the One of whom it is said,

> Behold, the tabernacle of God is among men, and He shall dwell among them, and they shall be His people, and God Himself shall be among them, and He shall wipe away every tear from their eyes; and there shall no longer be any death; there shall no longer be any mourning, or crying, or pain; the first things have passed away. And He who sits on the throne said, 'Behold, I am making all things new.' And He said, 'Write, for these words are faithful and true.' And He said to me, 'It is done. I am the Alpha and the Omega, the beginning and the end. I will give to the one who thirsts from the spring of the water of life without cost. He who overcomes shall inherit these things, and I will be his God and he will be My son'
> (Rev. 21:3-7).

> And there shall no longer be any curse; and the throne of God and of the Lamb shall be in it, and His bond-servants shall serve Him; and they shall see His face, and His name shall be on their foreheads (Rev. 22:3,4).

8

Peacemakers

Blessed are the peacemakers, for they shall be called
sons of God (Matt. 5:9).

Jesus is painting a beautiful picture of His disciples as He
describes these Beatitudes. Internally, they are a humble,
sensitive, conscientious people. They are 'poor in spirit,' they
are 'meek.' They 'mourn' their sin and'hunger and thirst for
righteousness.' They are the opposite of the proud, the
arrogant, the self-promoting, and self-assertive. As respects
righteousness, they are the opposite of the carnal, the
unconcerned, the flippant, the self-indulgent.

These essentially internal qualities have a profound effect
on how His disciples treat others. They are kind,
understanding, forgiving,'merciful,' straightforward, without
guile,'pure in heart,' sincere. He is describing wonderful
people, isn't He? We all aspire to be such. However, let's be
sure that we're not thinking that we must become such *before*
we can become Christ's disciples. As we noted at the outset,
these are not entrance requirements. Rather Jesus is describing
the ideals that His disciples are to pursue. These are primarily
matters of the heart. Only He can make us like what these
Beatitudes describe. Our response to them ought to be to
acknowledge our failure to be what He describes and cry out
for help. 'O Lord,' we ought to cry out. 'I am not these things.

Forgive my pride and lust and hypocrisy. Wash me in your blood. Cleanse my heart. Cause me to be born again. Make me a new person in Christ.' These may be clues for us that we are not real Christians. They are like the Ten Commandments in revealing our sin and showing us our need of the Savior. We could hope for nothing greater from our study of the Beatitudes but that we might come to know the true condition of our hearts and fly to the Savior to deliver us from ourselves.

This next quality, peacemaking, is dependent on those which precede it. R.T. France notes generally that,

> The absence of selfish ambition which has marked the earlier Beatitudes provides the only basis for this quality, which is particularly pleasing to God (111).

Stott sees a connection with that which immediately precedes it, purity or sincerity of heart, noting that 'one of the most frequent causes of conflict is intrigue, while openness and sincerity are essential to all true reconciliation' (50). In other words, there is a selflessness as well as a sincerity that is necessary if one is to be a peacemaker. Those who already have low opinions of themselves, who know their sin and mourn it, who know their hearts and are 'poor in spirit,' are the peacemakers. Those who are defensive or touchy, who are so thin-skinned and sensitive that they cannot be vulnerable and open, never can be. Similarly, those who are 'pure in heart,' who are not out for personal gain, who genuinely want the best for others, are peacemakers. Those who are double-minded, whose motives are mixed, who are insincere, or who approach life with a hidden agenda, cannot be.

Peacemaking

Who then are the peacemakers? 'He means those who use all their influence to promote peace and charity on earth, in private and in public, at home and abroad,' says J.C. Ryle (34).

They are 'people who end hostilities and bring the quarrelsome together,' says Leon Morris (101). Peacemakers are agents of reconciliation, spreading peace, harmony, and unity wherever they go. They are the opposite of troublemakers, who leave a trail of discord, conflict, and division. Jesus says, 'they shall be called sons of God.' They shall be 'called,' not here by God but by others, in the sense of being recognized as such or known as such. Why? Because in peacemaking they bear the image of God. God is 'the God of Peace' (Heb. 13:20). His Son is the 'Prince of Peace' (Is. 9:6-7). The gospel He preached is the gospel of peace (Eph. 2:17; cf. Is. 52:7; Rom. 10:15). The Father sent the Son in order to bring peace (Lk. 2:14). The apostles went about 'preaching peace through Jesus Christ' (Acts 10:36). The Apostle Paul writes,

> For it was the Father's good pleasure for all the fulness to dwell in Him, and through Him to reconcile all things to Himself, having made peace through the blood of His cross; through Him, I say, whether things on earth or things in heaven. And although you were formerly alienated and hostile in mind, engaged in evil deeds, yet He has now reconciled you in His fleshly body through death, in order to present you before Him holy and blameless and beyond reproach (Col. 1:19-22; cf. Eph. 2:11-22).

The Father aims to 'reconcile all things to Himself.' He makes 'peace' at great cost, 'through the blood of His cross.' We are 'reconciled' through 'death.' 'Those who make peace,' says Morris, 'are fulfilling what membership in the family really means' (101). Jesus is not so much teaching the doctrine of adoption, as in Romans 8:14ff., though that lies in the background. Rather He is indicating that which others will recognize is true of peacemakers. The peacemaking Father has peacemaking sons. Because reconciliation is at the top of God's agenda, it is at the top of His children's agenda as well. People will see the connection and respect it (cf. 5:16). The disciples of Christ have a zeal for peace, just like their heavenly Father. They 'seek peace and pursue it' (1 Pet. 3:11; cf. Ps. 34:14). They 'pursue peace with all men' (Heb. 12:14). They do everything they can to 'be at peace with all men' (Rom. 12:18). They are known to bring people together rather than to drive them apart.

Does this sound like you? Do you pursue with great zeal that which God purchased at great cost? Does peace follow you home, into the community and to the church?

Not Appeasement

We need at this point to distinguish legitimate peacemaking from appeasement. The peace advocated by Jesus and all the Bible is peace within the framework of justice and truth, not at the expense of it. Look back again at Colossians 1:19-22 and be reminded that the reconciliation and peace that is ours in Christ is not secured by denying that there is a problem, that we are sinners and alienated from God. Rather it is procured through His blood, through death. It comes at great cost in a manner consistent with justice and truth, that God might be both 'just and justifier' of those who believe in Jesus (Rom. 3:26). Furthermore, the reality of our situation must be fully acknowledged and admitted on those who receive forgiveness through costly repentance and submission to Christ. Peace comes only through fulfilling the requirements of justice, not suspending them.

As we've seen, there are those who cry 'peace, peace' when there is no peace (Jer. 6:14; 8:11). There is a superficial peace, a false peace which does not deal with the deeper, more difficult, more controversial, more potentially divisive underlying causes. Many so long for peace that they will accept it at any price. Leave things alone, they say. Let sleeping dogs lie. They never deal with the real issues, settling for a temporary truce rather than true peace. Such is not the policy of the godly but of the ungodly. It represents not admirable righteousness but moral failure. History's most notorious example of appeasement would have to be Neville Chamberlin stepping off a plane in London in September, 1938, having betrayed the Czechs to Hitler, waving a peace of paper in his hand, and announcing 'Peace for our times.' History went on to show that this was not peace but shameful compromise. More than that, it merely delayed the time of reckoning to a future date, made more terrible by the passage of time and the strengthening of the enemy. Churchill rose in the House of Commons to demand that the government tell the people the truth, saying,

> They should know that there has been gross neglect and deficiency in our defences; they should know that we have sustained a defeat without a war, the consequences of which will travel far with us along our road; they should know that we have passed an awful milestone in our history, when the whole equilibrium of Europe has been deranged, and that the terrible words have for the time being been pronounced against the Western democracies:'Thou art weighed in the balance and found wanting.' And do not suppose that this is the end. This is only the beginning of the reckoning. This is only the first sip – the first foretaste of a bitter cup which will be proffered to us year by year – Unless – by a supreme recovery of our moral health and martial vigour, we arise again and take our stand for freedom, as in the olden time (Manchester, *The Last Lion: Alone*, 371).

Peacemaking, whether political or religious, must take place within the framework of justice and truth without compromising either. Churchill understood this, Chamberlain did not. One may not claim the title of peacemaker if one denies the gospel in order not to offend people of other faiths. Such a policy may make for effective ecumenism but it is not biblical peacemaking. Jesus said he came not to bring peace but a sword, setting even family members against one another (Matthew 10:34-37). While He no doubt was speaking of effects not designs, he was describing the conflicts encountered by otherwise peace-loving and peacemaking Christian people. The gospel divides. Become a Christian and you are in for a fight with the devil, the world, and your own flesh. We don't make peace by giving in to them. The peace purchased at the cross is a costly peace, as also is all subsequent peacemaking. It does not come cheaply if it is the real thing. We don't make peace by silencing disturbing but important truths. One doesn't keep the peace in church by pretending that membership vows haven't been taken, or at home by pretending that marriage vows haven't been taken. A parent who stuffs candy into the mouth of a tantrum-throwing child, or one who surrenders car keys in order to silence teenage hysteria is not a peacemaker. A political leader who advocates compromising the rule of law and the requirements of justice in order to avoid the 'trauma' of an unsettling and divisive judicial process is not a peacemaker either. In each case one may have temporarily restored order. Yet 'peace' in each case is superficial and temporary. In each case there are battles that must be fought and won, and until they are, there will be no true peace. A church that compromises the gospel in order to please a member who threatens to withhold his contributions is not making peace, but rather guaranteeing future and worsening conflict, producing a series of decisions which may turn the church into a morgue, leaving the peace of a cemetery but no life. It is crucial that we be clear on this. Years ago a friend made a little sign for my desk that sits there still today – 'Peace if possible, but the truth at any rate.' Luther said that over 350 years ago and it is still true today. We long for peace, strive for peace, we work for peace, but not at the expense of justice and truth; not peace through cheating and lying. 'We must not so seek the flower of peace,' says Thomas Watson, 'as to lose the pearl of truth' (208).

True peace is much more difficult to achieve than we may have thought and therefore peacemaking is much more difficult to accomplish. Ultimately we find peace only in Christ. Reconciliation to God happens only when we recognize the hard truth about ourselves – that we are sinners, poisoned by pride, hypocrisy, and lust who must repent and cast ourselves upon Christ for mercy. This means absolute and unconditional surrender to Him. Consequently a peacemaker will not compromise this message. He won't water it down. Rather he will boldly proclaim it. However, the result may be that while many will find peace, many others will be offended. There will be conflict, alienation, and division. But we cannot therefore compromise our message, patching things up with happy words, baking cookies, or writing sweet notes. We mustn't repeat the mistake of the prophets who were content to heal the wounds of God's people 'slightly' (Jer. 6:14). No, all true peacemaking must have as its aim leading others to Christ the Prince of Peace. Only in Him will they find peace with God. Only when they have peace with God will they experience peace in their hearts. Only when they are at peace within will they be able to make peace in their relationships, and wherever they go.

True Peacemaking

How then is peace to be promoted?

First, one makes peace by being at peace with oneself. There is no course on peacemaking that will make one a peacemaker. Granted that if one took such a course or attended a seminar or conference on peacemaking one might hear some helpful things. But until one's heart is at peace one will continue to respond to the various situations of life in ways which make trouble not peace. To make peace one must be at peace. How does one come to have peace within oneself? By receiving the peace of God in Christ. Where there is a soul in turmoil, where there is internal conflict and discontent, it will spill over into relationships with others. Those who constantly have trouble swirling around them are invariably unsettled or discontent or even miserable within. We can state categorically that the primary problem for every troubled soul is alienation from God. The key to it all then is making peace with God. 'There is no peace for the wicked,' the Bible warns (Is. 57:21).

But in Christ we can have peace. 'Having been justified by faith we have peace with God' (Rom. 5:1). 'There is therefore now no condemnation for those who are in Christ Jesus' (Rom. 8:1). Because we know that we have 'peace with God' and are no longer 'under condemnation' we experience peace in our hearts. The big questions have been answered. A calm settles over us. We are given 'the peace of God which surpasses all comprehension' (Phil. 4:7). This provides a foundation for calmly and fairly dealing with others. Peacemakers are at peace within. They have heard Jesus say,

> Peace I leave with you; My peace I give to you;
> not as the world gives, do I give to you. Let not
> your heart be troubled, nor let it be fearful
> (Jn. 14:27).

And again,

> These things I have spoken to you, that in Me you
> may have peace. In the world you have tribulation,
> but take courage; I have overcome the world
> (Jn 16:33).

A few years ago I heard Dr Gutzke tell the story about a boy who was brought by his mother to his office so that he would 'straighten out' the young man. Apparently he was constantly getting into trouble and was a continual source of heartache for his mother. The boy walked in with a huge chip on his shoulder and sat down defiantly, daring Dr Gutzke to say something that would have an effect on him. Instead, Dr

Gutzke looked across his desk and said, 'Look, I know you don't want to be here and that you have no intention of listening to anything that I have to say, and I'm a very busy man, so why don't you just sit there and I'll sit over here at the desk and do my work, and after about an hour your mother will come back and pick you up and you can go on about your business and I'll go on about mine. How's that?' The young man said that he thought that sounded pretty good. So Dr. Gutzke went about his work. After about a half an hour, he glanced out of the corner of his eye and could see that the young man looked miserable. Calmly he looked up from his notes and said to him, 'My cup runneth over, how about yours?' Remarkably, the boy emotionally and spiritually crumbled. 'I'm miserable,' he admitted. Before long Dr Gutzke had led the young man to Christ. His life was changed. No longer was he a trouble-making boy who was a constant source of concern for his mother. He found peace and so became a source of peace.

A right relationship with God then is the key to peace in our hearts and to peacemaking. Knowing Christ puts an end to the inner turmoil and misery that disrupts relationships. Peace with God does away with the self-absorption that blinds one to the possibilities of peacemaking. Peace in our hearts provides a foundation from which to make peace with others. Ask yourself, are you at peace within? Are you at peace with God? Have you resolved the big questions of life? Have you banished the inner turmoil and pain that plagues so many? Only then will you be a peacemaker.

Second, we make peace by keeping the peace.

A significant portion of peacemaking has to do not with actively doing anything, but with just leaving things alone. A peacemaker often need not actually take positive action, but merely refrain from disturbing the peace. I find myself constantly telling my children – stay out of it! Leave it alone! But everywhere the troublemaker goes, trouble follows him. At every turn he finds conflict, disruption, and division. Why is

115

this? It is difficult to discern and one does not wish to attempt to psychoanalyze. But first there is discontent with himself and others. This then spills over into distrust of the decisions of others. The troublemaker believes only in himself. He knows it all. He has no confidence in the judgment or leadership of others.

Because he is discontent, he sows the seeds of discontent. He judges the actions and intentions of others severely, and shares his opinions widely. He spreads a bad report of others. He breeds ill will. He stirs up mistrust and conflict. Yet he is often hypersensitive about himself, easily offended, and deeply embittered. Because of his insecurities he may even recruit others into his group, thereby dividing the church or organization into factions. He must have others who agree with him, who see things as he does, who can validate his dissension.

The peacemaker, on the other hand, has a responsibility to preserve peace. How does he do this? Let us elaborate.

1. We preserve peace by promoting agreement.
The Apostle Paul writes,

> Now I exhort you, brethren, by the name of our Lord Jesus Christ, that you all agree, and there be no divisions among you, but you be made complete in the same mind and in the same judgment (1 Cor. 1:10).

We preserve peace by seeking to be of one mind, by sitting down with our Bible open, seeking understanding until we reach a consensus. How much consensus? As much as possible. We are to aim at shared convictions, aims, and goals. The great error of the ecumenical movement in this century is its failure to understand the theological foundation of the church's unity. We can never be one if we don't agree regarding who God is, the nature of the human problem, what Christ accomplished, how one is saved, and what the church is called to do. Only when we 'all agree' and are of the 'same mind' and 'same judgment' will there be 'no division among (us).'

2. We preserve peace by practicing humble forbearance with one another.

Again listen to the Apostle:

> With all humility and gentleness, with patience, showing forbearance to one another in love, being diligent to preserve the unity of the Spirit in the bond of peace (Eph. 4:2,3).

Do you see the effort involved in this? With 'humility,' 'gentleness,' and 'patience' we are to show 'forbearance' in 'love,' with the consequence that we diligently work to 'preserve the unity of the Spirit in the bond of peace.' In other words, if we are to have peace we will have to put up with a lot from one another and overlook a lot. The Bible says love bears all things, believes all things, hopes all things, endures all things (1 Cor. 13:7). Love 'covers a multitude of sins' (Prov. 10:12). For marriage to work, much has to be overlooked. For me to serve you as pastor, much has to be overlooked. One of the biggest disappointments of my life and ministry is to observe how quickly friends, even those with whom you have enjoyed fellowship and worked for years, will believe the absolute worst about you.

I am also amazed at what people will repeat in the hearing of others, things which cannot but breed ill will. Perhaps in a moment of weakness a joke may be told about so and so, even perhaps told with great affection. This then will be repeated to the one about whom the remark was made in such a way as cannot but cause hard feelings. Why do it? Also sometimes a thing is said out of genuine concern for the welfare of another which involves a measure of criticism, and someone will repeat it back to the one being criticized! This is done knowing that the result cannot but be hurt feelings and damaged relationships. Proverbs says,

> He who covers a transgression seeks love, but he who repeats a matter separates intimate friends (Prov. 17:9).

Peacemakers are very sensitive about how a thing will sound in the hearing of those around them. They are careful not to repeat things likely to be misunderstood or cause conflict. Instead they are building bridges between groups and individuals, opening lines of communication, and fostering understanding. Are you keeping the peace or stirring up trouble between groups and individuals?

Third, we make peace by pursuing reconciliation.

Even as God's peacemaking was a costly endeavor, so our peacemaking efforts cost us a great deal. Yet as we have seen, we are to 'seek peace and pursue it' (1 Pet. 3:11; cf. Heb. 12:14). It is costly to love our enemies. Yet we are called to do it (Matt. 5:44). It is costly to seek forgiveness when we have been in the wrong (Matt. 5:23-25). It is embarrassing and humiliating. Yet we are called to do it. It is difficult to rebuke one who has wronged us or is otherwise trapped in sin. But listen to what Jesus says:

> Be on your guard! If your brother sins, rebuke him; and if he repents, forgive him (Lk. 17:3).

'Well I tried that,' someone says, 'and then they did it again. I give up on them.' No, read further.

> And if he sins against you seven times a day, and returns to you seven times, saying, 'I repent,' forgive him (Lk. 17:4).

It is difficult to play the role of the mediator in reconciling warring sides. I have found myself more than once hated by both sides for my trouble. Yet we are called to be agents of reconciliation. Jesus prayed for the peace and unity of His church (Jn. 17:11,21,23). He died on the cross in order to make that peace possible. 'Christ suffered on the cross that he might cement Christians together with his blood,' says Watson. 'As he prayed for peace, so he paid for peace' (211).

Have you pursued reconciliation? Are you doing all that you can do to promote peace and unity in the church, and especially in your own personal relationships in the church? This is the work of peacemaking, undertaken by all who are children of God.

9

Persecuted for Righteousness

Blessed are those who have been persecuted for
the sake of righteousness, for theirs is the kingdom
of heaven. Blessed are you when men revile you,
and persecute you, and say all kinds of evil against
you falsely, on account of Me. Rejoice, and be
glad, for your reward in heaven is great, for so
they persecuted the prophets who were before you
(Matt. 5:10-12).

We arrive at last at the eighth and final of the Beatitudes,
and find that it is as surprising as the rest. Those who are
'blessed,' who are approved and favored by God, are those
who are 'persecuted' for the sake of 'righteousness.' Once
again, this is not what we would have expected. Not the
powerful and popular, but the oppressed, ridiculed, and
persecuted disciples of Christ are approved by God. Like
the rest, this is a mark of the true disciple of Christ.
Persecution is as much a mark of the Christian as is purity of
heart, peacemaking, or any of the others. 'All who desire to
live godly in Christ Jesus will be persecuted,' says the Apostle
(2 Tim. 3:12). The true Christian will suffer persecution in
one form or another.

Most of us are not going to greet this as good news. We
don't much like the idea of being 'revile(d),' a term meaning
to reproach or insult, or being 'persecute(d),' which takes us

beyond words to actions. A life in which all sorts of people are expressing 'all kinds of evil' against us, that is, making a great variety of destructive comments about us, is not appealing. But Jesus says that such are 'blessed' and ought to 'rejoice and be glad' about it.

How can this be? The disciples of Christ have a different view of life. They do not see things as the world does. Their motivation is different. The things that comfort and satisfy Christ's disciples are not like those which fulfill worldlings (5:4,6). They are motivated by the promise that 'theirs is the kingdom of heaven,' that 'they shall see God' (5:3,8,9). Their hearts, in other words, are set on eternity not the present age. They are seeking first God's kingdom and righteousness (6:33). They look not upon the things which are seen, which are temporal, but the unseen which are eternal (2 Cor. 4:18). They don't love the world or the things of the world. They are not seduced by 'the lust of the flesh, the lust of the eyes and the boastful pride of life,' because they know that these things are 'passing away.' They are motivated by the knowledge that the one who does the will of God 'abides forever' (1 Jn. 2:15-18). They have an otherworldly focus. Their hearts are set on eternity. Consequently, persecution in this world doesn't count for much. It just doesn't matter to them. 'Let goods and kindred go,' they say in the words of Luther's great hymn.

> That Word above all earthly pow'rs,
> no thanks to them, abideth;
> The Spirit and the gifts are ours
> through him who with us sideth.
> Let goods and kindred go, this mortal life also;
> The body they may kill: God's truth abideth still;
> His kingdom is forever.

This is a remarkable perspective. We look now at Jesus' words more closely.

Why Persecution

Why are the disciples of Christ persecuted? Why would persecution be so certain that it could be listed among the marks of the genuine disciple?

We'll start by clarifying what Jesus is not saying. He is not saying they are blessed who suffer for the sake of *unrighteousness*. There are times when we suffer the self-inflicted consequences of poor decisions that we have made. Because we are promiscuous or become intoxicated or are dishonest or cheat we sometimes suffer severely, even for years. For years we may suffer from disease, injuries, criminal records, fines, and damaged relationships. This is not suffering for righteousness' sake. It's just suffering. We have seen business leaders and politicians serve time behind bars because of their misdeeds. They suffer there terribly. Remember the aftermath of David's sin with Bathsheba. God forgave the guilt of the sin but there were temporal consequences, including the death of a child, rape of a daughter, fratricide, and civil war. David suffered enormously (2 Sam. 11ff.). But was it suffering for the sake of righteousness? Of course not. It was suffering for the sake of sin. It wasn't *persecution*, it was *punishment*. On a smaller scale, we sometimes say things we ought not to say and do things we ought not to do and end up alienated from former friends, alone, isolated, distraught, and miserable. Once again, this is suffering for the sake of foolishness or even outright evil, not for righteousness. There is no blessing promised in connection with this sort of suffering. As Peter says,

> By no means let any of you suffer as a murderer,
> or thief, or evildoer, or a troublesome meddler;
> but if anyone suffers as a Christian, let him not
> feel ashamed, but in that name let him glorify God
> (1 Pet. 4:15,16).

There is no virtue in suffering as a 'murderer' or as a 'troublesome meddler.' The suffering that is blessed and rewarded is that which is endured for the sake of righteousness.

Neither is Jesus saying that they are blessed who are persecuted for the sake of *self-righteousness*. Sometimes we may suffer because people react against our spiritual or moral pride, our judgmentalism, or because we lack tact, or wisdom, or sensitivity.

There are busybodies who rush in and make declarations, pronounce judgments, running over the tops of folks and stirring up considerable resentment in the process. This may be what Peter means by a 'troublesome meddler.' When the inevitable backlash comes, they claim 'persecution' as a badge of righteousness. But the fact is that others are reacting not to their righteousness, but self-righteousness: their tactless, insensitive, and untimely judgments and pronouncements. They're not standing for righteousness. They're merely being offensive. Sure, they stir up resentment. Yes, people are mad at them. Yes, they suffer. But not because they're righteous, rather because they're busybodies, because they're 'troublesome meddlers.'

Also cloaked in self-righteousness, though in a different way, are those who are persecuted for the sake of *non-righteousness* or *non-conformity*. There are some who reject not so much the moral standards but the customs and fashions and standards of the community, secular or religious, to which they belong. A disapproving response follows. They then congratulate themselves, imagining themselves bold defenders of individual expression and freedom as they turn up barefoot at a wedding, or wear immodest clothing, indulge in offensive language, or assault some other custom. As eyebrows are raised they reckon themselves persecuted for the sake of their righteous defense of personal liberty! I remember a caller on talk radio complaining that ever since he had divorced his wife and married his girlfriend the people at the church had been cool toward them. The hostess gave the very wise counsel that one ought not to join a communion that doesn't believe in divorce and then complain when you break the rules and suffer the consequences. Have you acknowledged your wrongdoing, the hostess asked? Have you taken the steps for restoration (all religions have such) that your religious body requires? Why then demand that everyone else compromise their standards in order to accommodate your selfishness? This is not suffering for righteousness, it is suffering for selfishness, self-centeredness, and pride.

Don't join an orthodox synagogue and then complain about the dietary restrictions. Don't join the Roman Catholic Church and complain about its prohibition of artificial birth control. Don't join a traditional Presbyterian church and complain about its strict view of the Christian Sabbath. Don't make a martyr out of yourself and call everyone else Pharisees and hypocrites. Don't cast yourself as a righteous defender of liberty and individual expression and brand everyone else as legalists. Don't cloak a rebellious streak in the garments of self-righteous martyrdom. I grew up in the capitol of non-conformity, Southern California. Non-conformity took on an almost religious status, as all standards in dress, grooming, speech, and social customs were overthrown. We congratulated ourselves as champions of individual expression, liberating society from the stifling uniformity of the 1950s. In retrospect I can see now that we were nothing of the sort. We actually were arrogant social anarchists, overthrowing and destroying customs and practices that for decades had protected society from vulgarity. I know the mentality and the self-deception and arrogance it involves. Ask yourself, Am I one who must always test the limits? Do I enjoy bucking the system and especially then complaining about any disapproving reaction that results? Jesus is not blessing those who suffer for the sake of rebellious non-conformity. The same thing can be said about many other forms of self-generated suffering. But I'm sure that you get the picture.

If these forms of suffering are not what Jesus had in mind, then what does He mean? He indicated His meaning with two phrases. He speaks of being persecuted 'for the sake of righteousness' and 'an account of Me' (vv 10,12). J.C. Ryle says, 'He means those who are laughed at, mocked, despised, and ill-used, because they endeavor to live as true Christians' (34). He has in mind those who both follow Christ and aim to be like Christ. In other words, the Christ-like life, lived in submission to Him, lived with Christ-like humility, purity, holiness, and godliness attracts attention. Such a life is resented. Such a life stirs up the fury of the world.

It needs to be said that this has always been the case. Jesus says, 'for so they persecuted the prophets who were before you.' Why? Because a righteous life, even without a word being said, convicts and condemns the world for its lifestyle, priorities, and pretensions. Ever thus has the world responded to the righteous with rage. From the very beginning there have been two humanities, the people of God and the people warring against God. There was Cain and there was Abel. Cain killed Abel. Why? The Apostle John answers that question:

> Because his deeds were evil, and his brother's were
> righteous (1 Jn. 3:12b).

There was Lamech and there was Seth. There was Noah and the rest of the humanity. There was Israel and the nations. There is the church and the world today. Sometimes persecution will come from outside the church and sometimes it will originate from within. Examples of external persecution might be that which Israel suffered in bondage in Egypt; the early church suffered at the hands of the Roman empire; the twentieth century church suffered at the hands of the Communists and Fascists, and the mission church has suffered almost wherever it has gone, whenever it has gone there, since the time of Christ. But sometimes the harshest persecution has come from those within the ecclesiastical community. Jeremiah had his Passhur, 'chief officer in the house of the Lord' (Jer. 20:1), who had him beaten, put in stocks, dropped into a cistern, and threatened with his life (Jer. 26:8; 38:1ff.). Jesus had his Pharisees, Paul his Judaizers, the Reformers their Papists, the Puritans and Covenanters their Prelates, the Great Awakening revivalists their unconverted opponents.

The severity of reaction can range all the way from, 'you bother me,' to torment and murder. Jesus does not detail the 'why' of persecution, He merely establishes the fact that it will certainly happen. Make no mistake about it. Do not be surprised. Among the several signs of the disciple of Christ is persecution. Later Jesus said,

> If the world hates you, you know that it has hated
> Me before it hated you. If you were of the world,
> the world would love its own; but because you
> are not of the world, but I chose you out of the
> world, therefore the world hates you. Remember
> the word that I said to you, 'A slave is not greater
> than his master.' If they persecuted Me, they will
> also persecute you; if they kept My word, they
> will keep yours also. But all these things they will
> do to you for My name's sake, because they do
> not know the One who sent Me (Jn. 15:18-20)

It also needs to be said that the world's hostility is unprovoked. The world will 'hate' and 'persecute' you just as they hated and persecuted me, Jesus says. Why? Because you are 'not of the world. You do not share the values, the interests, the desires, the outlook, the lifestyle of the world. You are different. The world views that difference as sometimes humorous, sometimes annoying, sometimes infuriating, and sometimes requiring your destruction. But the thing to notice is that hate lies at the bottom and there is nothing that you have to do to cause it. We've already seen that sometimes we provoke persecution. Sometimes it's our unrighteousness, sometimes our self-righteousness, and sometimes our provocative non-conformity – not our righteousness – that gets us into trouble. But the fact remains that even when we don't do a thing to bring it on, still the world hates both Christ and His people. 'They hated me without a cause,' Jesus said, citing Psalm 35:19 (Jn. 15:25). Likewise, without cause they both hate and persecute the Christian church.

Are you accustomed to thinking in terms of this antithesis? The world apart from Christ hates and would destroy the God of the Bible and all who are associated with Him. The Bible teaches us to think in terms of absolute antithesis. There is a God and God's people. Then there is the rest of the world, the enemies of God. The Bible allows for no middle ground. James asks,

> You adulteresses, do you not know that friendship with the world is hostility toward God? Therefore whoever wishes to be a friend of the world makes himself an enemy of God (Jam. 4:4).

Do you see that there is no middle ground, or for that matter, common ground? If you are 'friendly' with the world, that is, if you partake of the world, thinking like the world, playing like the world, working like the world, in effect, adopting a worldly way of life and so fitting in and conforming to the world, you are hostile, even an 'enemy' of God! The antithesis is absolute. The Apostle Paul says,

> Do not be bound together with unbelievers; for what partnership have righteousness and lawlessness, or what fellowship has light with darkness? Or what harmony has Christ with Belial, or what has a believer in common with an unbeliever? Or what agreement has the temple of God with idols? For we are the temple of the living God; just as God said, 'I will dwell in them and walk among them; And I will be their God, and they shall be My people' (2 Cor. 6:14-16).

Paul identifies two, and only two humanities. There are 'believers' and 'unbelievers'; 'righteousness' and 'lawlessness'; 'light' and 'darkness';'Christ' and 'Belial';'God' and 'idols.' These two are at war with each other. They can have no 'partnership' or 'harmony.' They are not to be 'bound together.' They have nothing in 'common.' They have no 'agreement.' 'Do not be conformed to this world,' says the Apostle Paul,'but be transformed by the renewing of your mind' (Rev. 12:1,2).

Consequently the world everywhere and always attacks the disciples of Christ. Peter says,

> Beloved, do not be surprised at the fiery ordeal among you, which comes upon you for your testing, as though some strange thing were happening to you (1 Pet. 4:12).

To be subjected to a 'fiery ordeal' is not a 'strange thing' for a believer. It is normal. It is ordinary. We are to expect it. Paul says,

> And indeed, all who desire to live godly in Christ Jesus will be persecuted (2 Tim. 3:12).

There is not a might or perhaps or maybe about it. The godly will be persecuted. Polycarp at the age of eighty-six was burned at the stake for refusing to call Caesar 'Lord.' Ignatius, another of the church Fathers, was thrown to the lions in the Colosseum. Listen to William Barclay's description.

> All the world knows of the Christians who were flung to the lions or burned at the stake; but these were kindly deaths. Nero wrapped the Christians in pitch and set them alight, and used them as living torches to light his gardens. He sewed them in the skins of wild animals and set his hunting

dogs upon them to tear them to death. They were tortured on the rack; they were scraped with pincers; molten lead was poured hissing upon them; red hot brass plates were affixed to tenderest parts of their bodies; eyes were torn out; parts of their bodies were cut off and roasted before their eyes; their hands and feet were burned while cold water was poured over them to lengthen the agony. These things are not pleasant to think about, but these are the things a man had to be prepared for, if he took his stand with Christ (I, 112).

Of course it didn't stop with Rome. The Inquisition on the continent and the Wars of Religion waged against the Protestants of France, Germany, and Holland brought terrible, horrible suffering. The English Puritans and Scottish Covenanters similarly suffered at the hands of the British monarchs and their ecclesiastical agents. Indeed, of the latter, Daniel Defoe, famous for his novel, *Robinson Crusoe*, said that the suffering of the Covenanters was worse than that endured at any time in the history of the church. In the twentieth century more Christians were martyred than in all the rest of the history of the church combined.

If this all comes as a shock to you perhaps it is because you have allowed yourself to take an overly benign view of the world. There is really no excuse for it at the beginning of the twenty-first century. Popular culture today is utterly hostile toward and destructive of Christian faith. Maybe back in the 1950s one might have thought that our civilization was neutral or even positive toward evangelical Christianity. Of course it actually never was. But at least it wasn't overtly hostile and so one might be excused for not knowing. But what excuse might one offer today for one's ignorance? The media, the government, the schools, the courts are all belligerent. All of our major institutions are hostile to orthodox Christianity. Our culture is relativistic and pluralistic and consequently hostile to anyone who is an absolutist and particularist. Do you still doubt that we're seeing this right? Are we overstating the case? Well then let me challenge you to a test. Devise some means – a poster, a letter to the editor, a speech to a social club – of proclaiming basic, essential Christian moral or religious teaching, and then wait for the response. For example, declare today that monogamous heterosexual marriage is the only legitimate outlet for sexual expression. Imply by doing so (as you must) that all other such range from the sinful to the perverse to the abominable. What will the response be? Or declare today that Jesus is the only truth and only Savior of the world and imply by doing so that all other religions are false and misleading. Can you predict the response? You will be scorned. The only sin our civilization universally recognizes is that of intolerance, defined as not believing that all beliefs and lifestyle practices are equally valid. Say that there is one way or one truth and you have committed the worst 'sin' that you can commit today. Yet this is precisely what each Christian must believe, proclaim, and defend. Consequently, persecution will inevitably follow. You will be ridiculed. You will be socially ostracized. You will feel the pressure to conform to the fashions of the day. You may be denied a promotion. You may lose your job. We've seen it happen. You may be rejected by your family. Ask any recent convert from Judaism or Islam about that.

What if I am not persecuted, not at any level at all? What does that mean? It could only mean one thing. This is difficult to say. But the facts all point in one direction. You must have made peace with the world. You fit in. The world doesn't know you except as one of its own. You must dress like the world, talk like the world, work like the world, play like the world, live like the world. You must be enough like the world to be accepted by the world. No, you won't be persecuted if you seem to have the same beliefs, values, priorities, perspectives as they do. You are seen primarily not as a disciple of Christ but as a part of accepted worldly society.

This does not mean that we need to go out and try to cause trouble. No, trouble is inevitable. The disciples of Christ will be persecuted. They cannot avoid it. But if I have managed to avoid it, where has the breakdown occurred? What am I doing that I shouldn't? What ought I to be saying that I'm not? What needs to change?

Why Rejoice?

Jesus tells us that the fact that we are being persecuted for the sake of righteousness, or on account of Him, is a cause for celebration. 'Rejoice and be glad,' He says (5:12). Impossible, you say. How could one be glad about such a thing? Not only is it not impossible to rejoice in persecution, but it is a lesson that the apostles learned well. After one occasion when they were arrested, flogged, threatened, and released we read,

> So they went on their way from the presence of the Council, rejoicing that they had been considered worthy to suffer shame for His name (Acts 5:41).

They rejoiced! They considered their suffering a privilege. Listen to the Apostle:

> For to you it has been granted for Christ's sake, not only to believe in Him, but also to suffer for His sake (Phil. 1:29).

What has been 'granted'? What is this great gift? To suffer! This is our privilege. Again Paul and Silas were attacked by a crowd in Philippi, arrested illegally, beaten with rods (inflicting 'many blows'), thrown into prison, and their feet placed in stocks. Yet we read that 'about midnight Paul and Silas were praying and singing hymns of praise to God' (Acts 16:25). This is remarkable and a great challenge for us. I'd rather sit and sulk. I'm more likely to claim status as a victim and seek to attract as much pity as I can. Why do they rejoice? Why ought we to rejoice? Jesus gives us two reasons, each preceded by the word 'for.' We'll take them in reverse order.

First, we rejoice because persecution is a sign of authenticity.

'For so they persecuted the prophets who were before you.' You are in good company. You are on the right side. You stand with them on the right side of history. You are numbered with the prophets as one of God's true servants. You are one of them, or at least one with them. You may not ever have the applause of the world. But you do have approval where it counts. Persecution is a badge of honor, placing one in the company of the prophets of God, who are approved and blessed by God.

I wonder if the experience of military boot camp or fraternity and sorority initiation week doesn't provide some insight into the intended effect of Jesus' words. Among the goals of army and fraternal initiation is the forging of a new identity for the initiates, as one of the few, the chosen, the best who have endured the hardships of the process. The initiates have what we have come to term a 'bonding experience' with one another, as well as with all who have gone before them. This is why one finds enduring, lifelong bonds between fraternity members and army buddies. Each is a brotherhood (or sisterhood) of suffering and shared knowledge. Their shared experience is a source of identity and pride.

Paul can speak of 'the fellowship of His sufferings' and mean very similar things (Phil. 3:10). The persecuted Christian is by his suffering initiated into a brotherhood of suffering. This brotherhood or fellowship includes the prophets, John the Baptist, Jesus Himself, the apostles, and all true believers through the centuries. This is the source of our identity, our pride, our joy. We stand with them. We are numbered among the true servants of Christ. We rejoice that we have received

133

such an astonishing privilege – to stand with those great saints who also were persecuted for the sake of Christ!

Continuing the parallel, do you remember, or can you imagine the joy when initiation week was over, and you had survived, and were initiated or commissioned or inducted (as the case applies) and made a part of the organization? No longer were you a plebe. You belonged. You were part of a larger group made up of all those who had survived initiation week. A profound sense of satisfaction and pleasure swept over you. This is the impact that Jesus' words need to make upon us. 'Theirs is the kingdom of heaven,' He says. Remember the emphatic tone of these Beatitudes. 'Theirs and theirs alone is the kingdom of heaven.' The kingdom of heaven belongs to them and to no others. The suffering of persecution for the sake of Christ initiates us into a fellowship of suffering that places us alongside those favored and approved of God, through the centuries, even with those whom God calls 'my servants the prophets.' This is to color the way that we look at our persecutions and persecutors. Sure, you are rejected by society. Sure you are in the minority. Yes they do scorn and ridicule and even seek to destroy you. But you are approved by God. You stand with the prophets. The fact that you are persecuted demonstrates that this is so, that you are the real thing. Is this not cause for rejoicing? It is one thing to be inducted into a sporting Hall of Fame. What an honor it would be to stand side by side with all those great stars. It would be wonderful to be elected President or Prime Minister and stand alongside all those great men who have gone before. But how much greater it is to be numbered with God's prophets, whose work is approved not just by the fans or historians, but by God Himself!

Second, we rejoice in persecution because eternal reward is promised.

'Theirs is the kingdom of heaven,' Jesus says. 'Rejoice, and be glad,' He continues, 'for your reward in heaven is great.' The reward Jesus promises is not meager, but'great.' Though the debasement of the English language has all but emptied the word'great' of its weight so that everything today is 'great,' from french fries, to the ball game, to the sale at the mall, what God calls 'great' is truly 'great.' There will be a greatness of reward both in quality and quantity, in what is given and how much is given. Great rewards will be given out of His infinite storehouse of treasure. We are not given many details on what exactly will be given but the fact of reward is certain. Jesus frequently mentions reward (e.g. Matt 6:4; 6:6; 6:18; 10:42; Lk.6:35). This should not be confused with merited or earned payment. Remember Jesus said,

> So you too, when you do all the things which are
> commanded you, say,'We are unworthy slaves; we
> have done only that which we ought to have done.'
> (Lk. 17:10).

He has in mind instead 'a freely given recompense, out of all proportion to the service (19:29; 25:21,23)' (France, 112). It is more like what we call a 'bonus,' a gift over and above one's pay that the giver is under no obligation to give. It might be like me asking you to help me move, and when we had removed the last stick of furniture, handing you the keys and saying,'Here, my former house is yours.' I would not be paying you. I would be rewarding you with a 'great' reward for faithful service. God is the 'rewarder' of those who 'seek' Him (Heb. 11:6; cf. 1 Cor. 3:10-13; 2 Cor. 4:17,18; 5:10; Heb.10:34; 11:27). The Psalms say,'Surely there is a reward for the righteous; surely there is a God who judges on earth!' (Ps. 58:11). What is that reward? God says of Himself,'I am your shield, your very great reward' (Gen. 15:1). We will receive what is alternately called a crown of 'life'of 'glory,' and an 'incorruptible' crown (Jam. 1:12; 1 Pet. 5:4; 1 Cor. 9:25; cf. Rev. 4:10).

The reward, let it be noted, is 'in heaven.' Much as we

might like to see it now, it is not promised now but then, in eternity, in heaven. This is not to say that there are not rewards for Christian discipleship in this world. There are indeed. I don't believe that there is any life worth living but that which is lived 'in Christ.' In Him we find the answers to the eternal questions, the forgiveness of our sins, reconciliation with God, eternal life, peace, joy, and direction for all the questions of living life in this world. But for all that, the promised reward is in heaven, not here. This means that often the perception will be that Christians lose and the bad guys win in this world. Righteousness seems to go unrewarded. The righteous get trampled while the wicked go on unpunished, not only getting away with their evil, but actually thriving because of it (see Pss. 37;73). God doesn't settle accounts in this world. 'We hope for what we *do not see,*' the Apostle Paul writes (Rom. 8:25). 'Faith,' says the writer to the Hebrews,'is the assurance of things hoped for, the conviction of things *not seen*' (Heb. 11:1). We don't see the reward of the righteous and punishment of the wicked in this world. Stars and starlets who do vulgar and immoral things, athletes who cheat, politicians who lie, businessmen who steal all seem to get away with it. Christians, who follow Christ and live righteously, in the meantime are persecuted, reviled, mocked, ridiculed, and slandered. Where is God in all of this? He is in heaven, with His reward. In Him, Jesus has promised, we'll receive comfort (5:4), satisfaction (5:6), mercy (5:7), sonship (5:9), even the earth (5:5), even God Himself, whom we shall see (5:8). 'All things belong to you,' says the Apostle Paul (1 Cor. 3:22). In the meantime we live like Moses,

> choosing rather to endure ill-treatment with the people of God, than to enjoy the passing pleasures of sin; considering the reproach of Christ greater riches than the treasures of Egypt; for he was looking to the reward (Heb. 11:25,26).

Are there the 'passing pleasures of sin'? Yes, of course there are. There is no use denying it. The sins of the flesh and their benefits can be enchantingly pleasurable. Do we endure 'ill treatment'? Of course we do. We have seen in detail that there is a cost, a price to be paid for Christian discipleship. But this we consider as 'momentary, light affliction' (2 Cor. 4:17). We consider 'the reproach of Christ' to be 'greater riches,' a greater honor, a greater privilege, a greater purpose or goal for life than mere 'passing pleasures.' We too, like Moses, are 'looking to the reward.'

10

Responding to the Beatitudes

It remains for us now to draw concluding lessons underscoring the importance of these beautiful virtues that we have called 'Beatitudes.'

First, we have seen the priority that Jesus places upon the condition of the heart.
All of the Beatitudes, singularly and collectively, describe the condition of the heart of the one who is approved or favored by God. This is a lesson not to be missed. It is the heart that is described, not the conduct. God is not as concerned with external behavior as He is with internal spiritual condition. Hypocrites can conform externally to the lLw while still being filled with anger and lust (5:21-32), dishonesty and hate (5:33-48). They can pray and fast while becoming filled with spiritual pride and ambition for worldly recognition (6:1-18). They can claim to believe while laying up treasures on earth, while serving God and mammon, while being consumed with anxiety about life and its provisions, and while seeking *second* the kingdom of God (6:19-34). The behavioral demands of the Bible can be faked. This is why the Sermon on the Mount begins with the Beatitudes. God wants from us *pure* hearts (5:1-12), *whole* hearts (in our obedience, 5:21-48), *undivided* hearts (in our piety, 6:1-18), and *trusting* hearts (6:19–7:6). I cannot settle for external

conformity to legal demands. I cannot turn Christianity into moralism. God wants my heart.

Interpreters, beginning at least with Luther and many commentators since, have emphasized the impossibility of fulfilling the Beatitudes. We cannot refashion ourselves after their ideal image. As we have noted repeatedly, what we need are new hearts. The Beatitudes point out our need of the new birth (Jn. 3:1 ff.). We must be united to Christ in His death and burial and raised up in newness of life (Rom. 6:1 ff.). We must become new men with new hearts, new 'creatures' in Christ Jesus, the old things passing away and all things becoming new (2 Cor. 5:17; Rev. 21:5). We need as well, the ongoing, indwelling, filling, and empowering of the Holy Spirit to continue the work of refashioning us in the image of Christ (Eph. 5:15 ff.; Rom. 8:4–14; Gal. 5:16–26). We are not adequate for these things (2 Cor. 2:16–3:6). He must supply all our needs (Phil. 4:19). Only by His grace are we sufficient (2 Cor. 12:9) and do we become what He wills for us to become (1 Cor. 15:10). Our prayer is that of the Psalmist,

> Create in me a clean heart, O God, And renew a steadfast spirit within me (Ps. 51:10).

The call to persistent prayer in Matthew 7:7–11 underscores these truths.

Second, we have seen the interrelatedness of the Beatitudes.

We should not aim at one to the exclusion of the others. We should understand that they rise and fall together. The Christian is one who is deeply aware of his spiritual bankruptcy, his weakness, and unworthiness, and so is 'poor in spirit.' Consequently he 'mourns' his spiritual condition, grieving over his personal sin as well as evil in the world around him. Because he understands what he is not – he is not righteous, not worthy of heaven, not deserving of blessing, not capable of pleasing God – he is 'meek,' that is, lowly and humble before God and man.

These three largely negative descriptions of the Christian's self-awareness flow into positive responses. He longs to be other than he is and so he 'hungers and thirsts after righteousness.' He knows his need of mercy and so he shows mercy, he is 'merciful.' His dealings with others are straightforward, without guile, from the heart, and pure. Having peace, he makes peace. Being persecuted, he retains joy.

The Beatitudes are a description of the whole person. They flow from one to the other and will not easily be divided. One could hardly be 'poor in spirit' and yet not be 'merciful' in the face of weakness of others. One could not 'hunger and thirst after righteousness' and not 'mourn' one's sin. One could not be 'pure in heart' and not be 'meek.' They hang together. Like the fruit of the Spirit of Galatians 5:22 ff., they are in a sense singular. They describe the virtues or graces of the true disciple. Together they present the target at which we are to aim in our war against the flesh (Gal. 5:13 ff.; Rom. 7:14 ff.) in our goal of Christ-likeness (Phil. 2:5 ff.).

Third, we have seen how the Beatitudes are the key to the rest of the Sermon on the Mount and to all of that which God expects of us.

Formulas, programs, 'three steps,' 'five stages,' and 'ten secrets' are not the key to Christian discipleship. 'Success' in marriage, family, child-rearing, finances, work, Christian mission, and everything else flows from character. If the heart is right, everything else eventually falls into place. If the heart is not right, nothing else can become or remain right. This is proven, it seems to us, by the verses that follow the Beatitudes in the Sermon on the Mount. As we said at the outset, Christian influence flows from Christian character as smoothly as verses

13-16 flow from verses 1-12. Having described the Beatitudes, Jesus immediately identifies His disciples as 'salt' and 'light.'

> You are the salt of the earth; but if the salt has become tasteless, how will it be made salty again? It is good for nothing anymore, except to be thrown out and trampled under foot by men. You are the light of the world. A city set on a hill cannot be hidden. Nor do men light a lamp, and put it under the peck-measure, but on the lampstand; and it gives light to all who are in the house. Let your light shine before men in such a way that they may see your good works, and glorify your Father who is in heaven (Matt. 5:13-16).

These two metaphors describe the impact that Christian character has upon the environment in which it is placed. Salt flavors, preserves, and prevents corruption. Light dispels darkness and illuminates. The result is Christian fruitfulness in the lives of unbelievers as they 'see (our) good works, and glorify (our) Father who is in heaven.'

The 'good works' of the Christian are then elaborated in Matthew 5:17–7:29, that is, in the rest of the Sermon on the Mount. We are to obey the whole law of God, down to the 'jot and tittle,' keeping and teaching even the least of them (5:17-20). Our righteousness is to exceed that of scribes and Pharisees in that we conform to God's Law both internally and externally. Our hearts are to be rid of murderous hatred and anger (5:20-26), and of adulterous lust, even cutting off the offending hand and plucking out the offending eye (5:27-32). Our words are to have integrity, our yes being yes and our no being no (5:33-37). We are to love our neighbors and our enemies, turning the other cheek, giving the coat off of our backs, walking the extra mile. This is what our heavenly Father does, sending His sun to shine and rain to fall on the righteous and unrighteous. Because He is the standard, we are to be perfect as our Father in heaven is perfect (5:38-48).

Our practice of religion is likewise to be from the heart, aiming at pleasing God, not calculated to be seen by men.' We are not to 'sound a trumpet' when we give, or 'stand on street corners' when we pray, or put on gloomy faces when we fast. Our piety is to be practiced in private for an audience of One, our Father who is in secret (6:1-18).

We are to live a life of faith, not laying up treasures on earth, not attempting to serve God and mammon. We are to trust God, not being anxious about life, about what we shall eat and drink and wear. Trusting His daily provision we are to'seek first the kingdom of God and His righteousness' (6:19–7:6).

All this flows from the heart. The Beatitudes are the key to all the rest. Do they not summarize all that we truly seek? If so, they will shape our commitments. We will persistently ask, seek, and knock for them in prayer (7:7-11). We will stick to the narrow gate and way and the few who walk there. We will beware of false prophets and false professors of Christ who say'Lord, Lord' but who do not do the will of the Father in heaven (7:13-23). We will build our lives solidly on the rock of Christ and not on the shifting sand of worldly wisdom (7:24-27).

The tragic decline of the Christian church in the West is a grievous phenomenon for God's people to contemplate. Strenuous and commendable exertions have been made by the Christian community to reverse this trend and bring the multitudes to Christ, restore the church, and repair the Christian family. But we are attempting what never can or shall be if we imagine that gospel revival is possible through a therapeutic message, innovative technique, and improved organization and management. The same might be said of those who imagine that the establishment of a neo-Puritan ministry will usher in a golden age of fruitful ministry comparable to that of the sixteenth and seventeenth centuries. Spiritual health and fruitfulness flow from character. The sharp bite of salt, its abrasiveness, its sting, is the bitter taste of Christian character as prophetic witness. Whatever we may preach, the foundation of salt's corruption - fighting and righteousness - preserving witness is the godliness of hearts stamped by the Beatitudes. This is what preserves marriages, families, churches, and even nations. Whatever we may proclaim from our pulpits or across our backyard fences, the foundation of our gospel is the light of our good works that flow from good (or pure) hearts. This is what illuminates a world lost in the darkness of religious and moral falsehood, error, and confusion. This is what shows the way forward, what illuminates the narrow path of life for the individual, the family, the church, and the nation. The light and salt of righteous character are the key to the fruitfulness, the 'success,' the impact of gospel ministry in our day and in every era. This is not to say that content (what we proclaim) and form (how we say it) are without importance. It is merely to recognize what must come first. It is to distinguish the foundation from the superstructure.

These, it seems to me, are the three crucial lessons of the Beatitudes. Really these lessons are but one. Our God will never settle for disciples whose allegiance is external, formal, or mechanical. He insists upon disciples of the heart. These, and these alone, are 'blessed' by Him. These alone are authentic. These alone overcome the world in which they are placed.

Bibliography

Barclay, William. *The Gospel of Matthew – Vol.1 (Chapters 1–10)*.
Philadelphia, Pennsylvania:
The Westminster Press, 1958.

Boice, James M. *The Sermon on the Mount*. Grand Rapids, Michigan: Zondervan Publishing House, 1972.

Bonhoeffer, Dietrich. *The Cost of Discipleship*.
New York, New York: MacMillan Publishing Company, Inc., 1959.

Burroughs, Jeremiah. *The Saints' Happiness*.
Ligonier, Pennsylvania: Soli Deo Gloria Publications, 1660, 1988.

Carson, D.A. 'Matthew' in *The Expositor's Bible Commentary – Vol.8*.
ed. Frank E.Gæbelein, 1-599.
Grand Rapids, Michigan: Zondervan, 1984.

Ferguson, Sinclair B. *Kingdom Life in a Fallen World*. Colorado Springs, Colorado: Navpress, 1986.

France, R.T. *Tyndale New Testament Commentaries – Matthew*.
Grand Rapids, Michigan:
Eerdmands Publishing Co., 1985.

Henry, Matthew. *A Commentary on the Whole Bible – Vol.5*.
Iowa Falls, Iowa.
World Bible Publishers, 1721, *n.d.*

Hill, David. *The Gospel of Matthew*. New Century Bible.
Grand Rapids, Michigan: Eerdmans;
London: Marshall, Morgan and Scott, 1972.

Keener, Craig S. *A Commentary on the Gospel of Matthew*.
Grand Rapids, Michigan;
Cambridge, UK: Eerdmans, 1999.

Lloyd Jones, D. Martyn.
Studies in the Sermon the Mount, Vol.1.
London, England: Inter-Varsity Fellowship, 1959.

Morris, Leon. *The Gospel According to Matthew*.
Grand Rapids, Michigan:
Eerdmands Publishing Co., 1992.

Pink, Arthur W. *An Exposition of the Sermon on the Mount*.
Grand Rapids, Michigan:
Baker   Book House, 1950, 1982.

Plummer, Alfred. *An Exegetical Commentary on the Gospel
According to St. Matthew*.
Grand Rapids, Michigan:
Eerdmans Publishing Company, 1910, 1953.

Ryle, J.C. *Expository Thoughts on the Gospels – Matthew*.
Cambridge, England:
James Clarke & Co. Ltd., 1856, 1974.

Stott, John R.W. *The Message of the Sermon on the Mount*.
Downers Grove, Illinois:
Inter-Varsity Press, 1978.

Tasker, R.V.G. *Tyndale New Testament Commentaries –
The Gospel According to St. Matthew*.
Grand Rapids, Michigan:
Eerdmans Publishing Company, 1961.

Watson, Thomas. *The Beatitudes*.
Edinburgh, England:
The Banner of Truth Trust, 1660, 1971.

Persons Index

Aaron, 58
Abba Father, 51
    see also God
Abel, 126
Africans, 77,89
Agrippa, King, 54
Apostle John, 28,52,79,126
Apostle Paul, 34,66,68
    cleansing ourselves, 102
    critiqued Judaism, 98
        eternal rewards, 52,55,136
        fleeing sin, 76
        friendship with the world, 128-
    129
        grieving, 41-44,46,55
        inheriting
            the kingdom, 104-105
            the new earth, 60
        life of, 32-33
        peace, 116-117
        persecution, 53-
    55,121,127,132-133
        pleasure, 38
        poverty of spirit, 27,32
        purity of heart, 97
        reaping what one sows, 87
        reconciliation through
        the cross, 109
        repentance, 49
        suffering for
        righteousness, 132
        testing, 129
        the meek, 64-65
        thorn in the flesh, 27
apostles, 27,32-33,41,50
        persecution, 54,132-133
        preached peace, 109
Augustine of Hippo, 8
Aylward, Gladys, 86
Barclay, William, 58,129
Bathsheba, 43,123
Belial, 128-129
believers, 23,79,106,128-129,133
        'fiery ordeal' for, 129
        unbelievers, 64,128-129,142
Beloved, the, 129
'blessed', the, 14,22-23

body of Christ, 79-80
brethren, the, 79,116
bride of Christ, 80
Burroughs, Jeremiah, 22
Caesar, 129
Cain, 126
Calvin, 61,91
Carson, D.A., 11-12,21-22,26,29,59,96,103
Chafer, Lewis Sperry, 11
Chamberlain, Neville, 111
child of God, 43,45,51,54,110,119
Chinese, 86
Christ, 40,45,73-74,77,79-80,91,103
        answers eternal questions, 136
        became a curse, 35
        believing in, 132
        blood of, 110
        bore our sins, 35
        'bread of life', 74
        Christ-like, 64,75,78,106,126,141
        commitment to, 99-100
        contrasted with Belial, 128-129
        cross of, 42,81,119
        crucifixion, 67,106
        death and resurrection, 45,77,140
        disciples of, *see* disciples
        divinity, 26
        hated by the world, 44,128
        His bride, 80
        His church, 79
        honor and glory of, 17
        image of, 140
        in heaven, 52
        knowledge of, 78,82,103,115
        life as a ransom, 35
        living a godly life in,
    21,32,44,121,129,136
        'living water,' 74
        love of, 77,80
        mercy in, 87,113
        multitudes come to, 143
        name of, 18
        need for, 35,73
        new creation in,
    80,82,105,108,140
        no condemnation in, 51,114
        peace in, 109-110,113-115
        persecuted for, 55,134,136

Subject Index

Scripture Index

Terry Johnson is the Senior Minister of the historic Independent Presbyterian Church in Savannah, Georgia, USA. In 1993 he was named the convenor and then chairman of the PCA General Assembly committee on Psalm-singing. Among the fruit of their labours was the *Trinity Psalter*, of which he was the editor and compiler. He has also published *Leading in Worship*, a source-book for Presbyterian ministers, and *The Family Worship Book*, a resource book for family devotions (the latter published by Christian Focus Publications). He is married to the former Emily Billings and they have five children.

Other Books
from
Christian Focus
By
Terry Johnson

When Grace comes Home

How the doctrines of grace change your life

Terry Johnson

How does 'Grace' become a part of your life so that God becomes real to you in every situation?

'Terry Johnson has provided a splendid work on how right theology bears upon our worship, character, suffering, witness and growth in the Christian life. 'whether evangelicals know it or not, their future as a viable movement depends upon the rediscovery of such God-honoring theology.'

**Thelate Dr. James M. Boice,
Tenth Presbyterian, Philadelphia**

'Rarely can the vitamin content of sweet, strong, classic pastoral Calvinism have been made so plain and palatable as it is here.'

**J. I. Packer,
Regent's College, Vancouver**

'Terry Johnson… enriches our understanding of the difference that the doctrines of Grace not only make to the way we do theology, but also for the ways in which we serve God and love our neighbors'

**D.G. Hart, Associate Professor of Church History,
Westminster Theological Seminary**

'The fine book proves for Christians something that they should already know, but often miss: theology matters! With much practical wisdom and help for Christian thinking and living, this book makes good application of good theology.'

**Rev. Dr. Robert Godfrey,
Westminster West Theological Seminary**

ISBN 1 85792 5394

The Family Worship Book

A Resource book for Family Devotions

Terry Johnson

Do you struggle to provide enjoyable, meaningful and spiritual times of family devotions? Do you avoid the whole subject but have the nagging thought that you should be doing something? Here is the solution, a book that will give you the impetus to start.

Terry Johnson (who gave us Leading in Worship) has now provided us with a superb resource for family religion: The Family Worship Book. Johnson provides a brief but compelling argument for the importance of family worship, but then takes those he has convinced in theory to the next step: actually putting it into practice!

In a day and age when family worship is a rarity, and in which parents who are called to lead in it are not likely to have had personal experience of it in their own upbringing, Johnson's book will prove to be an invaluable aid. I have known many parents who feel the responsibility to lead the family in devotional exercises and who genuinely desire to be faithful in that covenantal responsibility, but who do not seem to know what to do or how to begin.

Here's the antidote. I hope that this book will be widely circulated and used among God's people. We may not expect a climate of serious spirituality to return to our churches until family religion again becomes a norm. May the Lord use this book to bring about a revival of family worship in our land.'

J. Ligon Duncan, III
First Presbyterian Church, Jackson, Mississippi
Adjunct Professor of Systematic Theology,
Reformed Theological Seminary, Jackson, Mississippi

ISBN 1 85792 401 0

Christian Focus Publications

We publish books for all ages. Our mission statement -

STAYING FAITHFUL
In dependence upon God we seek to help make his infallible word, the Bible, relevant. Our aim is to ensure that the Lord Jesus Christ is presented as the only hope to obtain forgiveness of sin, live a useful life and look forward to heaven with him.

REACHING OUT
Christ's last command requires us to reach out to our world with his gospel. We seek to help fulfil that by publishing books that point people towards Jesus and for them to develop a Christ-like maturity. We aim to equip all levels of readers for life, work, ministry and mission.

Books in our adult range are published in three imprints.

Christian Focus contains popular works including biographies, commentaries, basic doctrine, and Christian living. Our children's books are also published in this imprint.
Christian Heritage contains classic writings from the past.
Mentor focuses on books written at a level suitable for Bible College and seminary students, pastors, and other serious readers; the imprint includes commentaries, doctrinal studies, examination of current issues, and church history.

For a free catalogue of all our titles, please write to:
Christian Focus Publications, Ltd
Geanies House, Fearn,
Ross-shire, IV20 1TW, Scotland,
United Kingdom
info@christianfocus.com

For details of our titles visit us on our website
www.christianfocus.com